Inspiration From Anytown, USA

Inspiration From Anytown, USA

Florence, Alabama

STWL :

A good

College Friend.

Bill Norvell

Bill Norvell

ISBN: 1507769164
ISBN 13: 9781507769164

This book is dedicated to all who value true friendship.

Please join us in friendship that I believe is best expressed by James Triplett, one among the 30 individuals featured, who said it best in his cross-stitch sampler of the quote by Albert Camus that reads:

Don't walk in front of me,
For I might not follow.
Don't walk behind me,
For I might not lead.
Just walk beside me,
And be my friend.

Acknowledgements

A sincere thanks to the thirty individuals who trusted me to share a tiny portion of their stories. Your willingness to participate and your genuine concern for helping others filled me with gratitude. By getting to know each of you, my life has been forever changed for the better. I truly value your friendship.

To Charlotte Tomlinson Homan, my advisor during this endeavor ; Your calm disposition and your unique gift to offer encouragement at precisely the right time proved to be invaluable. Your unwavering faith and humility has been a blessing and an inspiration to me.

To Michelle Rupe Eubanks, my remarkable editor; I asked you to make it hard on me, and did you ever oblige. But without your keen attention to detail, this undertaking would never have come to fruition.

To Cliff Billingsley: Your creative skills in photography greatly enhanced the final product.

To my son, William Norvell: You initially sparked in me a desire to act on my vision.

To my wife, Anne: You put up with the mood swings I endured throughout the writing of this book.

Lastly, and importantly, to all of my friends in the world of social networking. Someone once said, "Facebook friends are phony. They aren't real." Well, that person was badly mistaken. Many of you heard about this project and consistently offered words of support and encouragement. We need a community of support, and I'm blessed to call each of you my friend.

Table of Contents

Introduction

While sitting on a bench in downtown Florence, Alabama, on April 5, 2014, a young man approached me and said, "I've got to leave this town; there are no interesting people here." I tried to convince him otherwise, but he brushed me off and walked away. Within a few minutes, a vision came to me suggesting I feature thirty interesting local people – fifteen men and fifteen women – in an inspirational book. The purpose is to inspire, encourage, and help others through the shared life experiences of these individuals. The two qualities sought during the selection process were authenticity and humility. The end result is what you hold in your hands.

While none of the people were selected on the basis of their faith, a common theme emerged during the interview process. Each individual stressed that his or her faith has been an important part of their lives. Some, of course, were more willing than others to share their beliefs.

My intent was never to share any portion of my story when this endeavor began. As I listened to their stories, however, I realized a desire to share something that I had never revealed to anyone.

The story begins simply enough. My family of four was enjoying life in beautiful Greenville, South Carolina, in 1990 as I worked as a supervisor for one of Crawford and Company's 400 United States office locations. The ultimate goal for me was to become a branch manager for one of these sites. The phone call came in the summer of 1990 when I was offered the opportunity in Waycross, Georgia. While hopeful the opening might have been Huntsville, Alabama; Nashville, Tennessee; or another exciting city, I accepted the job in South Georgia, sight unseen.

When travelling with my family to Waycross for a house-hunting trip, my wife, Anne, cried as we surveyed the depressed and desolate town. This was an old railroad community, and, while the railroad had dried up, the residents soldiered on. The culture shock of leaving the gorgeous Greenville area to move to swampy Waycross seemed unimaginable.

Before the trip, I had some idea of what I was getting us into with this move. I'd met with my boss and had seen that the performance results of the Waycross office placed it last in all measurable categories among all United States locations. I told my wife this news, and she cried even harder. Even worse, we didn't know a single person in the town that would soon be our new home.

I became angry – angry at my boss, angry at the town, and angry at the world. Why me? I wondered. Why was I being sent to this desolate area in the middle of the Okefenokee Swamp? I hadn't a clue. But I had accepted the job, and there was no turning back.

We placed our Greenville home on the market, and while Anne and our two boys waited for it to sell, my home for the next fourteen months was the low-budget Pine Crest Motel just off the main drag in town.

Prospects of improving the Waycross office were dismal. The town appeared desolate, and business conditions were highly unfavorable. After six months of trying to improve office efficiency, nothing was working. Things just got worse. I was acutely aware that managers of poorly performing locations didn't keep their jobs too long. I was an emotional wreck, unable to eat, unable to sleep, and frankly, unable to think.

But on March 1, 1991, something unusual took place while I was picking at a fried chicken lunch inside room 125 at the Pine Crest. The motel maid, Emma Jones, whom I had come to know, came inside to clean my room. I unloaded on her about Waycross being a miserable place to live. Emma, an African American woman of forty-five, listened calmly to my complaints.

About ten minutes later, this woman whom I knew to be the youngest of thirteen children, spoke and said, "Mr. Bill, you has to have faith. God will provide."

Initially, I dismissed her remarks as nonsense. What does she know about business? She doesn't understand my problems. But Emma wasn't finished with me yet.

Before leaving the room, she said, "Mr. Bill, you must accept Jesus into your life." She then gave me a smile and left to complete her duties.

Being a person of little faith at the time, her advice seemed comical. My thought was to hurry back to the office and back to the disaster that it was. But since there was nothing to do, no real work to get back to, I remained inside the tiny motel room that was costing me seven dollars a day. After what seemed like hours of contemplation, I reluctantly heeded Emma's advice. What was there to lose, after all?

I got down on my knees in the tiny motel room and accepted Jesus into my life. I must admit to feeling a bit silly and embarrassed after praying to God for guidance and support. This was not me. The idea of telling someone, or anyone, about this moment never occurred to me. While difficult to explain, I began to feel a calming come over me, as if things just might be okay.

But nothing changed during the next six months. Our condo wouldn't sell, my office remained a financial nightmare, and I was still living in number 125 at the Pine Crest Motel.

However, not too much later, my wife called with some news.

"The condo sold," she said. "We're moving to Waycross."

I wasn't sure whether to cheer or to cry. How would my family adapt to Waycross after living in Greenville? Further, where would we live? My salary at the time was such that we couldn't afford a house in any respectable neighborhood.

The following day, a local agent called me and said, "Bill, will you come by the office to discuss doing some business."

After securing him as a client, we experienced a slow but steady improvement in office efficiency. Anne, the boys, and I found a house in a nice area for $49,000. It was a three- bedroom home in an area with paved roads. Was this the turnaround for which I'd prayed?

While my family was unhappy with me for the first year, they slowly began to appreciate the genuine nature of the people in this South Georgia town. The residents were caring, compassionate, and real. They were good folks, and if any petty cliques existed, we never saw them. We came to love the town and its people.

After five years in Waycross, a phone call again changed our lives. I was offered the management position in, of all places, my hometown of Florence, Alabama. We moved to Florence and have lived here since. My oldest son, David, is a graduate of the University of North Alabama. My youngest son, William, is a Coffee High School graduate and a graduate of the University of Alabama and the Stanford Graduate School of Business.

My career, seemingly at a dead end in 1990, continued for the next eighteen years. I was blessed to work with outstanding employees in Florence; Tupelo, Mississippi; and Huntsville, Alabama.

Upon reflection, the turning point in my career and in my life took place in the most unlikely of places. It occurred in room 125 in a tiny motel on March 1, 1991, in the heart and soul of South Georgia. And in hindsight, the high point of my thirty-three year career was living and working in Waycross.

Both of my sons have said to me on many occasions how much they disliked me for moving to Waycross but how it later became the best thing to happen to them.

I'm still awaiting my wife's confession.

One other unusual event occurred in my life on Sunday evening the 24th day of February in 1991, just before this special lunch conversation with Emma Jones the following Friday. After spending the weekend with my family in Greenville, I was driving back to my tiny hotel room in Waycross to begin another week filled with stress and worry. My mind was wandering while driving on the desolate Highway 82 leading from Tifton to Waycross, and my 1989 Ford Escort, a company car, seemed like the only vehicle on the flat and unfriendly highway.

I will never forget the feeling of aloneness; I have never felt this alone before or since. Suddenly, a flashing light of a Georgia State Patrol car appeared in my rearview mirror. Before pulling off the highway in pitch-black conditions at 10 at night, I noticed, as I slowed the car, that I was driving eighty-five miles-per-hour.

The patrolman demanded that I sit in his car while he wrote the ticket. He made a few unsavory remarks about my total disregard for the law. He was no-nonsense and rude. Frankly, I didn't blame him. I decided this was the final straw for me in South Georgia. I would call my boss the next day and resign my position. It was too hard. I would move back to Greenville with my family. I could get another job.

For reasons I don't understand to this day, after getting the ticket, I began pouring out my story to this middle-aged highway patrolman. After fifteen minutes of listening, the officer's attitude and demeanor toward me slowly began to change.

"Mr. Norvell, please slow down, and I sincerely hope and pray that you come to enjoy South Georgia," he said as he tore up the ticket he'd just written.

After this encounter, I drove on to my tiny and lonely room in Waycross. I'd decided that I couldn't quit after a stranger and an officer of the law had shown such concern about my well- being. The following Friday was the encounter that would forever alter my life.

I have often wondered how our lives are changed as a result of one tiny event or a choice made by us or others. If there is a message in these two unlikely events in my life, I believe it is that we must understand a higher power is in control.

This story would not have come to light had I not met the thirty people who willingly agreed to participate in this undertaking. Because of my reluctance to speak openly about my faith and because of embarrassment or fear of criticism, I refused to share this life-changing event that occurred twenty-five years ago.

I am grateful to the thirty people featured in this book for inspiring me to share my message. But more importantly, my sincere hope is that by reading their stories, you will be inspired to examine closely your life and your beliefs. My life has been richly blessed by getting to know each individual, and I hope this book will do the same for you.

Chapter 1

Norma Cassimus Glascock

Norma Glascock is a woman who believes that, through the power of love, we can solve many of the world's problems. She genuinely cares about people, and her intoxicating spirit is highly contagious. Norma learned this and many other things, not the least of which is her never-give-up attitude, from her Greek immigrant father and her deeply caring mother. She grew up in the Weeden Heights community of Florence, Alabama, and worked side-by-side with her parents in the family business, Cassimus Grocery Store and Café. While Norma has faced deep and personal loss throughout her life, she is included to remind everyone that, no matter how painful the issues, it's possible to find joy and fulfillment by taking life one step at a time.

Norma is the middle child of three daughters to John S. and Gertrude Coffman Cassimus, of Florence. Her down-to-earth parents were known around Florence for the family business, Cassimus Grocery Store and Café, which was a unique grocery store and café on Huntsville Road in the Weeden Heights community.

"My sisters and I grew up helping Mama and Daddy in the café," said Norma. "Daddy opened the store in the 1930s and ran it until he retired in 1986. His café was perhaps best known for serving chili, beef stew, and Daddy's popular half-and-half, which was a mixture of chili and beef stew. Hamburger steaks, hamburgers, hot dogs, and hot bologna sandwiches were also popular items on the menu. As much as customers raved about the food, it was the fellowship that most of them came to love about our cozy and friendly café."

Norma recalled the unique way in which customers would settle up at the end of a meal.

"Today, you get a bill at the table at the end of your meal. Well, customers at Cassimus Café never did," Norma said. "My younger sister, Pat Pace, always helped Daddy with the cooking duties while my older sister, Betty, and I took customers' orders. We never wrote down the orders, just memorized them, and gave them to Daddy in the kitchen. A bit surprisingly, I don't recall anyone complaining about getting the wrong meal. After lunch, the customers went to the cashier, which was my Mama, and simply told her what they'd had. Mama would then total up the bill, and they'd pay her. It was the honor system all the way."

Many loyal customers lived near the Cassimus family in Weeden Heights.

"The Weeden Heights community was a wonderful place to live," said Norma. "Some dear friends who lived nearby were the Flippo family and the Oldham family. Others were the Terry Richardson family, the Wylies, and the Garners. Mama and Daddy loved music, and we were fortunate to have many talented musician friends who also lived in the community. Someone was always playing an instrument and singing in the neighborhood. I remember the Green family and Jones Oliver coming by the store on many occasions. And Ronnie Flippo, a United States Congressman, never came home from Washington D.C., without visiting the café. It was probably because I set up his first date with his wife, Faye Cooper. Ronnie thanks me even today."

Norma spoke of being inspired by watching her father, whom she remembers as being a compassionate man and treating all customers the same, regardless of their social status, money, race, or religion.

"Daddy welcomed everyone, and they all loved the food and our soda fountain," Norma said. "I still remember how he treated each individual as an equal, and he never let anyone leave his store hungry, even if that person was unable to pay. Another fond memory is of riding with Daddy to deliver groceries to families. Those were the days. The way Daddy treated the less fortunate has stayed with me still."

In addition to her parents, Norma's maternal grandmother, Elizabeth Crunk Coffman, was a powerful influence in her life.

"Grandma moved in with us after my parents married," Norma said "She was a deeply spiritual person who read her Bible every day. People in our community called her Aunt Dolly, and she was every bit as strict as my parents. Grandma and my folks were among the original founders of Weeden Heights United Methodist Church. She was an excellent role model, and Grandma was responsible for influencing me spiritually. She was a special person."

Norma had one of those childhoods that's distinctly Southern American. Life was slower, maybe even easier. And, as a child and adolescent, Norma enjoyed a wonderful relationship with her parents and her two sisters that shade her memories of life in Weeden Heights.

"My folks closed the store every Wednesday at noon and took us for a drive or to the movies," said Norma. "They loved the movies, and, often, they took us to Decatur or Huntsville to see special features. I even remember them taking us to Birmingham on special occasions to see a movie. These are wonderful memories. At the store, Daddy let us trip the jukebox, invite friends inside, and dance until we wore ourselves out."

Norma graduated from Coffee High School in 1958 and soon thereafter married Fred Glasscock, who was from Tuscumbia, Alabama, and who also happened to be a serious cowboy.

"Freddy was part Native American and loved riding his horses," said Norma. "He was so scholarly. Freddy read his classics and loved his westerns. He was well-versed in Biblical history and loved to discuss events with anyone who was ready and willing. He was an incredible husband, father, and role model for our two children, Darryl and Beth."

Family was Norma's top priority in the 1960s and 1970s as she was busy raising her two children. But, in 1983, tragedy struck when husband, Fred, was diagnosed with pancreatic cancer.

"Freddy lived just a year after the diagnosis," Norma said. "He was thrilled to live long enough to see Beth graduate from Bradshaw High School in 1983. Darryl was at the

University of North Alabama at this time and helped me immensely during Freddy's illness. Beth, my daughter, who was also my best friend, knew she had to get on with her life after losing her dad. She left a few days after the memorial service to begin studies at the University of Alabama."

Life didn't stop for Norma, either. Just three months after Freddy died, Norma's mother passed away.

"It was really hard dealing with this much loss in the span of a few months," said Norma. "I helped Daddy a little bit at the café until a dear friend, Shelby Warren, suggested that I consider the real estate business. I got my real estate license and began a career with Coldwell Banker in 1988, and it's still ongoing. It was a wonderful decision, and I have loved helping people in this business."

Norma has always been an avid outdoorswoman and has a passion for spotting and photographing the bald eagle. She has been closely observing, photographing, and documenting the habits of bald eagles for more than thirty-five years.

"It's fascinating," she said. "This is my passion. My other passion is hiking. I've led many a hiking tour into the Sipsey Wilderness, which is a gorgeous area inside the Bankhead National Forrest. We pitch tents, cook over an open fire, and tell stories. It's an experience that will touch your heart and soul. I've also hiked the Tennessee portion of the Appalachian Trail."

What advice might she offer to others who are reluctant to venture into the wilderness?

"Many people create boundaries for themselves," said Norma. "I see young people consumed with the image of who they think they should be based on others' expectations. It's important to step outside your comfort zone. Be creative, hike, explore, and never be afraid to try something new. Discover what you care about, and translate it into the kind of life you desire."

Following her passion for the outdoors has helped Norma cope with the loss of other close family members. Her sister, Pat Cassimus Pace, and her daughter, Beth Glasscock Pflug, were diagnosed with cancer and fought courageous battles. Both succumbed to the disease, however, in 2012 and 2013, respectively.

Facing this pain and loss has been a battle in and of itself, Norma said, but she's learned ways to manage the grief, even while she admits it never goes away.

"It really hurts," she said. "It hurts so deeply, and the pain of losing a child is unimaginable. I think about my daughter every day of my life. I've found it's best to stay busy and continue living the best I can under the circumstances. While the pain never disappears, I've discovered it simply has to be managed. One helpful tool for me has been to wear something of Beth's every day. This is a way to honor her and keep her spirit close to me twenty-four hours a day. I'm wearing four of her items today. I miss her more than anything; Beth was my angel on earth."

Despite this loss, Norma goes to work with a smile on her face and exudes an astonishing energy level. She attributes some of this to a lifestyle change she made thirty years ago when she became a vegetarian. After watching a documentary on the treatment of animals at the time of slaughter, Norma vowed never to eat meat again. She has remained true to this promise.

"I felt deeply moved to change my life," said Norma. "The way animals are treated and slaughtered for processing will make you sick to your stomach. You will also discover, as I have, that you'll feel better after eliminating meat from your diet."

As one who has experienced the highs and lows of life, Norma felt inspired to share a few messages learned from the good times as well as from the pain of deep personal loss.

"Get outside in nature," she said. "You don't have to be athletic to watch bald eagles or go hiking. People ask me all the time, 'Where are the eagles?' I say, 'Just look up. They're everywhere.' We're fortunate to have many resident bald eagles in our community. As far as hiking is concerned, go to the library and learn about the activity. For beginners, I'd recommend the Cane Creek Canyon Nature Preserve in Tuscumbia, Alabama, or the Shoal Creek Preserve near Florence. If you really want an experience, call me and join me and a few friends on a hiking trip in the Sipsey Wilderness. You'll be glad you did. Most importantly, get moving, and do interesting things. It's amazing how many fascinating activities are at our fingertips in this community.

"At the expense of sounding corny, some of us just don't know how to have fun," Norma added. "I was fortunate Daddy taught me that it's okay to take time out from working hard to enjoy life. It's okay and important to stretch your boundaries and to learn new things, regardless of your age. From the days of dancing in the café with friends, I realize now, in hindsight, that Daddy was instilling in me a simple but important message. He said, 'Please don't miss the dance.'

"Finally, death leaves a heartache no one can heal, but love leaves a memory that no one can steal. And when you begin hiking in the wilderness, remember the words that Native

Americans have used for thousands of years as I believe they teach us an important lesson. The words are:

Listen to the wind, it talks.
Listen to the silence, it speaks.
Listen to your heart, it knows."

Chapter 2

Bill Batson

$\mathcal{B}$ill Batson is a person of unquestioned high moral character. In word and deed, Bill sets a standard for integrity. He has treated people with honesty and compassion throughout the ninety-two years of his life. While the former mayor of Florence, Alabama, moves a little slower than in the past, he hasn't lost a fraction of his kindness for treating people fairly and with respect. Bill is featured here because of his sterling reputation and commitment to doing the right thing.

Bill is the youngest of four children to Ezra and Mabry Batson, of Sylacauga, Alabama. He learned a great deal by observing the work ethics of his father, a businessman, and his mom, a teacher of voice and diction in the Sylacauga City School System. Raised in the Methodist church, it was a given Bill would attend Birmingham-Southern College. His tenure at the private liberal arts school would be a short one, however, as he spent many a late night at the famed Pickwick Club in Birmingham.

"The Pickwick Club was the hot spot for private parties and dances," said Bill. "It featured the big-band sound, a revolving glitter ball suspended from the ceiling, and the mechanical bull for all the crazies. I loved it when the Auburn Knights Orchestra, a jazz and swing big band based out of Auburn, played at the Pickwick. Sherrill Toomer, son of the owner of Toomer's Drugs in Auburn, was the front man for the band at this time. They were fabulous."

In hindsight, and after a few too many nights spent enjoying the Pickwick Club, Bill said, "I guess the University of Alabama was calling my name."

Bill hit the ground running in Tuscaloosa by declaring a major in business and accounting.

"I knew I best find work quickly in Tuscaloosa, because my dad was a bit upset with my weak academic performance at Birmingham-Southern," said Bill. "I auditioned for a local jazz band called the Alabama Cavaliers. I had played the saxophone in our high school band, and the Alabama Cavaliers offered me a chance to audition. They hired me as one of the saxophone players. We had four sax players, one trombone player, one trumpet player, and our rhythm section. A talented and beautiful girl was our lead singer. We played at fraternity and sorority parties and a number of private gatherings. It was fun but also hard work because our goal was to make money."

Being a member of the Alabama Cavaliers was just one of the jobs Bill had during his college career. He was also the circulation manager for The Birmingham News. This required him to pick up the newspapers at the bus station at 4:30 every morning, seven days a week.

"It felt like I was working all the time I wasn't in class," he said. "After getting the papers, I took them to the office to disperse to the twelve delivery boys. Many nights, I played a music gig and picked up the papers still wearing my tuxedo. The folks at the bus station didn't know what to make of me, but I suppose they had a good laugh at my expense."

After graduating from the University of Alabama with an accounting degree, Bill accepted a job in New Orleans, Louisiana, with Freeport Sulphur Company. At the time, he was engaged to his college sweetheart, but the relationship had already begun to unravel. The direction of Bill's life would change forever after a weekend visit to Sylacauga with his dad in 1947.

"I told Dad that my girlfriend felt she could get along fine without me," said Bill. "Dad asked me to drive him to Florence to see his brother, Adin Batson. Uncle Adin was the owner of the Corner Drug Co., on the corner of North Seminary and Tennessee streets in downtown Florence. Uncle Adin influenced me to move to Florence and set up shop as a public accountant. I did so and began picking up local clients."

It was a difficult undertaking to run a public accounting firm in 1947, and Bill learned that Louis Rosenbaum, father of Stanley, was seeking an accountant for his family business. At the time, the Rosenbaums owned all of the movie theaters in the Shoals and surrounding areas. Bill was offered and accepted the job in 1947. The Rosenbaum name is now associated with architecture as it was Louis's son, Stanley, who commissioned famed architect Frank Lloyd Wright to build the family home on Riverview Drive in Florence. It remains the only Frank Lloyd Wright-designed home in Alabama.

With his genteel sense of humor intact, Bill described Louis Rosenbaum as not the most handsome of men in town, but, for what he may have lacked in good looks, he more than made up for in generosity. After two months on the job, Louis gave Bill a ten-dollar-per-week raise and the office girls a five-dollar-per-week increase.

"The girls rushed downstairs and began hugging and kissing the elder Rosenbaum," Bill said.

But Stanley, also in the family business, approached Bill and said, 'You don't seem excited about the raise. Is it not enough?'

"No, it is more than I deserve," Bill replied. "But if you think I am going downstairs to kiss your daddy, you are crazy. The girls overheard my remarks and noticed Stanley going downstairs to talk to his father. I have never heard anyone laugh as loudly as Louis Rosenbaum," Bill said.

While working for the Rosenbaums, Bill was contacted by a close friend, George Morris, controller for Olan Mills, a portrait photography company based in Chattanooga, Tennessee, regarding a potential job as a travelling auditor. The job offered a company car, expense account, and the opportunity to see the country.

"Louis Rosenbaum actually told me it was the perfect time to make this move because I was single," Bill said. "I accepted the job in 1948 and travelled to thirty-two states while completing audits for the company operations. I came to know Olan Mills Sr., and his wife, Mary Mills, very well. All of my expenses were covered, so my paycheck went straight into my account at First National Bank in Florence."

After a year-and-a-half on the road, Uncle Adin Batson once again called Bill back to Florence. Uncle Adin asked Bill to consider becoming a business partner in his three drug stores.

"The road was getting lonely, so I accepted Uncle Adin's proposal to join him in business," Bill said. "This was in 1950 when I came back to Florence, and I am still here in 2015. After several years with Uncle Adin, it seemed best to consider returning to public accounting. My uncle bought out my interest, and I returned to my role as a self-employed public accountant."

Bill mentioned that, on the first day he was in Florence back in 1947, he met an interesting person at the local Chamber of Commerce.

"This was my first time to meet Clyde Anderson," Bill said. "He was serving as the chamber president when I first began practicing. Clyde was so genuine and down-to-earth. After I joined First United Methodist Church in downtown Florence, it was Clyde who convinced me to begin attending the men's Sunday school class. I am thankful for Clyde's persistence in getting me there every Sunday. I have loved being a member."

Bill learned an important lesson from a dear friend he came to know from this class, a person who would greatly impact his life.

"I prefer not to mention his name, but he shared a lesson with me on forgiveness," said Bill. "He told me that we should forgive even our most bitter enemies. He told me how he once went up to his most bitter enemy on the street in downtown Florence and said, 'I love you.' This one encounter, along with three words, changed the other person forever. These two men, previously bitter rivals, became and remained best friends for the rest of their lives. I learned that we must forgive."

Career building aside, Bill was itching to get married and start a family. One holiday season in the early 1950s would make this dream a reality. It was a Christmas Eve in 1954 that Bill spent in Huntsville, Alabama, that would bring other changes to his life. Bill's sister had invited the neighbors over for refreshments and among them was Louise Stone. Bill invited Louise, who quickly became known as Lou, to ring in the New Year with him at Florence Country Club, and that was the start of a beautiful courtship. They were married a year later, in 1955.

Bill became emotional when reflecting on his wife of fifty-seven years; she passed away in 2013. He recalled her sense of humor on a particular evening when he was receiving an award from the Florence Country Club.

"Lou said that evening that she thought being a member of a country club meant you were rich," said Bill. "Lou then said, 'Boy, was I mistaken.' Lou got the best of me that night."

Bill and Lou's life together was a happy one, and the family was enriched by their two children, Suzanne Batson Morris and Robby Batson. Needing some additional income to support his family, Bill decided to run for Mayor of Florence. His friends told him that he would never win because he didn't graduate from Coffee High School, the only high school in town at the time. But with a heavy dose of Sylacauga charm, he proved them wrong.

As Mayor, he faced many tough decisions on how best to run the City of Florence. He recalled one incident involving more than two dozen policemen. As city employees, policemen were banned by law from going on strike, so they decided to engage in a "sick in." The policemen contended they were sick and, therefore, unable to perform their duties as officers of the law.

As Mayor, Bill handled the situation with his usual characteristic charm and humor.

"'I am sorry you are sick,' I told them, 'But if you don't get well in two weeks, your job will be gone,' " Bill said. "I believe about twenty were so sick they no longer wanted to work for the city."

In his life, Bill has learned quite a few lessons about business and people.

"Be honest and upfront with people, and schedule time for dear friends," he said. "Maurice Cox and Miles Carter, my best friends, joined me every year on a trip to one major league ballpark. Those were special memories."

It was clear by the emotional strain on Bill's face how deeply he missed his departed family members and close friends.

"That's the toughest part of living so long," said Bill. "I'm still here, but many of my loved ones are gone. It never gets easier, and I miss them desperately."

Bill realizes that he is playing in extra innings of a remarkable and deeply satisfying life. He still attends meetings at the Florence Exchange Club, where he has been a member for sixty-two years. He frequently meets friends for breakfast, he reads extensively, and he loves baseball. Despite age-related illnesses and long-gone friends, Bill hasn't lost his zest for life and his uncanny sense of humor. His advice to others is as timeless as the man himself.

"It is easy to follow the crowd, but remember: The crowd can be wrong," said Bill. "As far as living a life of meaning, let me reflect on lessons learned when visiting the baseball parks with my dear friends. Many people search for meaning in all the wrong places and fail to touch the most important bases. You determine the important bases in your life. Be sure to touch every one of them."

Chapter 3

Noona Kennard

$\mathcal{A}$ pioneer is one who ventures into uncharted territory to settle an area; a trailblazer innovates by setting the path for others. Both descriptions fit Noona Kennard, but the last thing on Noona's mind when she arrived in Florence in 1950 was blazing a trail. She wanted to get rich and play ball. One day, however, she discovered that God had another plan for her life. Once Noona realized her purpose in life, she blazed a trail in a manner that forever changed female sports in the state of Alabama. She is included for this reason.

Mamie Dorothy Kennard was born at home in a big bed in the front bedroom at 401 Gillespie Street in Starkville, Mississippi, on Valentine's Day in 1928.

"My mother was two months pregnant with me when my dad, Arthur Kennard, died," said Noona. "While I never knew him, Daddy was a farmer, hunter, fisherman, and raised show turkeys. Our farm was a dairy and cotton farm located twelve miles from Starkville in the Oktoc community. Nine families lived on the farm, and, in exchange for their housing, food, and clothing, they ran the day-to-day operations. After Daddy died, my Uncle Everett, whom we called Brother, assumed the responsibilities of the farm. Uncle Everett slowly began teaching my brother, Boswell, how to run the farm. Boswell took over the farm, and he still lives there today."

Mamie, named for her mother, was a baby when she got the nickname that's still with her today.

"Shortly after I was born, my brother glanced at me and said, 'She has a little tongue. She's just a little Noona'," said Noona. "I've been Noona ever since."

Life on the farm was difficult on the widow, but family was always around to help, Noona said.

"My mother depended on her mother, Molly Boswell, who lived in nearby McCool, Mississippi, to help us after Daddy died," Noona said. "Mama, I called her, brought us vegetables from her garden every week and even paid my tuition when I later attended college. Our livelihood was derived from the Kennard farm."

Noona loved athletics from an early age, and it wasn't a surprise when she made the varsity basketball team as a freshman at Starkville High School. In fact, Noona became the first freshman to be voted to the All Little Ten Conference team, an award given to outstanding players on teams in the surrounding areas.

"We played six girls on a team, three guards and three forwards," said Noona. "Most people today have no concept of how girls' basketball was played in the early days. The forwards were the only players allowed to shoot the ball, and the guards just played defense."

When deciding on colleges, Noona chose Mississippi State College for Women, or MSCW, now known as the Mississippi University for Women, in Columbus, Mississippi. Referred to as the "W," this was an all-female institution at the time.

"I knew I wanted to play ball, and the 'W' offered me the opportunity," said Noona. "While pursuing my degree in physical education, I played basketball, volleyball, and participated in track and field. After getting my degree in 1950, I went to Tuscaloosa, Alabama, and took more courses in physical education. I would later claim my master's degree in physical education from the University of Alabama."

While at Alabama, a friend mentioned to Noona that there was a need for a physical education teacher for the junior high school in Florence, Alabama. J. W. Powell, Superintendent of Education for Florence City Schools at the time, and Tom Braly, Coffee High School principal, travelled to Tuscaloosa to interview candidates for the position.

"They must have liked me because they offered me the job on the spot," Noona said. "Mr. Powell said, 'Do you want the job.' I answered, 'Yeah.' My mother and my sister, Ruth, drove me to Florence in my uncle's pickup truck. I had no idea where I was going, but Mr. Powell found me a room to rent in the home of Mr. and Mrs. E. G. Prosser on Walnut Street. The Prossers were Christian people, and Mrs. Prosser's sister, Miss Claude Moore, lived with them as well."

It wasn't long before Noona heard about the delicious meals offered at nearby Starkey's Restaurant. She still remembers that first lunch there.

"Mildred Shaw, a teacher, who also lived in the Prosser's home, and I walked over to the restaurant," said Noona. "Just minutes after we were seated, the waitress brought us plates of food. We told her we had not yet ordered. She replied, 'That's all we got. Enjoy.' Well, it was good."

Noona realized one day early in her career how closely her students paid attention to her, even down to what she was wearing.

"Three girls passed me in the hall, and I smelled something," Noona said. "I asked them, 'What is that smell?' They replied, 'Tabu. Like you.' The Lord seemed to say, 'See? They will even copy your perfume – you need to get your life right. Invite me into your life'."

Noona, a lifelong Baptist, began attending First Baptist Church, which was just a stone's throw from the Prosser home, because she felt that all teachers should go to church.

"I was all about me and travelling the world to play ball until the Holy Spirit, through the preacher, awakened my spirit," said Noona. "When I accepted Jesus that Sunday in 1950, I came to realize that God sent me here to plant me. My life began to change. I no longer wanted to run; I wanted to plant."

During her first year in Florence, Noona realized that girls were not allowed to compete in athletics for their school teams in Alabama. This was contrary to what was offered for girls in Mississippi.

"I called the Alabama State Department of Education and was informed girls were not allowed to compete in sports in their school's name like the boys," she said. "However, we could field an independent team and use the school's facilities. This was great news to me."

With assistance from Simmons Electric, Dixie Sporting Goods, later Hibbett Sporting Goods, and Foote Olds-Cadillac, Noona formed a team called the Black Racers and, later, the Dixie Racers. One of her players was Nancy Kennedy Darcy; Nancy recalled seeing Noona help many girls deal with their own personal issues.

"Noona was the best when it came to helping young girls," said Nancy. "She has always been a wonderful person of sound Christian values. We played teams like Piney Chapel and Bill's Drive Inn from Huntsville. Bill's players were car hops, and they were as mean as yard dogs. Those were fun times, and Noona made a deep and lasting impression on every one of us."

Despite the exciting times of coaching the independent teams, Noona yearned to coach women's sports at the high school level. This opportunity came in 1955 when Neville High School in Monroe, Louisiana, offered her a job teaching physical education and coaching basketball and softball.

"I left Florence to pursue my dream," said Noona. "But after one year in Monroe, J.W. Powell called me and said, 'We need you back in Florence.' I loved that man, and I was positive that girls in Alabama could play basketball as well as girls in Louisiana, Mississippi, and Tennessee. I returned to Florence in 1956 more determined than ever to convince others of this."

After ten more years of no girls' basketball, in 1966, Noona was offered the job as physical education teacher for a new high school named Bradshaw. The following year, Joyce Tatum came to Bradshaw to serve as her assistant coach and physical education teacher.

"Joyce was my assistant in everything," said Noona. "Joyce coached other sports by herself and had great success. She won several state championships in badminton and archery. Joyce preferred to remain behind the scenes, but I would never have accomplished anything without Joyce helping me every step of the way. While I oversaw all sports, Debbie Anderson and later, Rosalie Stevenson, handled the coaching for our gymnastics team. But we were still told the gym was for the boys."

Eventually, however, that attitude about women in sports began to change, Noona said.

"My dream from Day One was that girls be given the opportunity to compete on athletic teams representing their schools," Noona said. "I kept bugging the powers that be but to no avail. Finally, after seventeen long years, in 1967, the Alabama State Department of Education held State Sports Days but only in volleyball and track and field. The girls could now compete in their schools' names. It later came to my attention that a few high schools had allowed girls to compete in swimming and tennis prior to 1967.

"Mabel C. Robinson, a leader in the Alabama State Association for Health, Physical Education, Recreation and Dance, supported this effort. Mabel came to visit me in Florence several times over the years. The State Sports Days were held at the University of Montevallo, and schools competed at regional sites to earn the right to advance to Montevallo."

These preliminary competitions were referred to as Play Days, according to Kennard.

"Our team didn't qualify for state that first year, and I was in the stands," said Noona. "As a spectator, I said to myself, 'I'll never sit here again, I'll have a team competing.' From then on, I had a team on the court, and I was coaching from the sideline. Several years later, the department of education changed the name State Sports Days to State Championship. Our team at Bradshaw became the first ever to three-peat as we won Class 4A state titles from 1971-1973. In 1979, Bradshaw hosted the State Volleyball Championship for all four school classes. In front of a sold-out crowd at the Bradshaw dome, we claimed the Class 4A state title, and the fans began to notice female sports."

Noona coached and taught at Bradshaw for twenty-one years until her retirement in 1987. During her tenure, Kennard won seven state championships in volleyball, two in track, and three in bowling. She and Joyce Tatum also coached golf, tennis, and softball for girls at Bradshaw.

Kennard's efforts were recognized by the Alabama High School Sports Hall of Fame in Montgomery when she was inducted as a member in 1993. When the inaugural class of inductees was honored by the newly formed Lauderdale County Sports Hall of Fame, Kennard was selected along with eleven other athletes and coaches.

Always blazing the trail, she was one among six women from across the United States to receive Coach of the Year honors for high school girls' sports in 1975. This award came after Kennard had first been named Coach of the Year for Alabama. While Kennard's home is filled with awards, she is quick to point out she never coached for recognition.

"I never did anything for awards," said Noona. "After I trusted the Lord, my life was forever changed, and I knew I was to coach and teach girls not only sports, but also about living a Christian lifestyle. If my efforts helped one girl, then I consider my career successful. I loved helping the girls. In return, those girls saved my life."

It's important to note that Noona also had an impact on sports for girls in her home-town of Starkville, Mississippi.

"I was playing in a women's softball league in Starkville in the summer of the early 1970s when Dog Owens, the Director of the Starkville Parks and Recreation Department, asked me to start a softball team for girls," said Noona. "I did so for young girls and am proud to say the Ponytail League I began is thriving even today."

Although Noona retired from her career as a coach and teacher in 1987, she has in no way retired from spreading God's message.

"I began Gospel Tees in 1984 before I retired," said Noona. "I knew I wanted to share with others how God changed my life and how He will change theirs if they are willing to accept Him into their hearts. My idea was to put God's messages on t-shirts and travel to meet people, sell the shirts, and let them get to know the Gospel. My dear friend, Freda House, has travelled with me to numerous craft shows in order to market our designs."

While the words on the shirts may vary, the message is always the same, Noona said.

"I've had many designs over the years," said Noona. "But, after using so many scripture verses, I decided on using John 3:16 on my items. Now, the front of my shirts reads: 'I'm A Whosoever.' This is one of the most widely quoted verses from the Bible. It reads: 'For God so loved the world that he gave his only begotten Son, that whosoever believeth in him should not perish, but have everlasting life.' "

After years in coaching, Noona has learned that nothing is better – in life or in sports – than a strong foundation.

"I believed in teaching fundamentals, and while I was honored to coach many outstanding teams, my first job was to teach physical education to the average girl," Noona said. "Without a strong foundation in sports or in life, you're not going anywhere. It's important to develop a personal relationship with Christ. Jesus had a team of twelve who were unsure of where they were going until three years later when the Holy Spirit entered their hearts. The same is true for us in life."

Noona Kennard came to Florence in 1950 and soon encountered huge obstacles, ridicule, and little support. She was told that girls were not athletes. But she soon realized that God had a plan for her life, so Noona forged ahead, and in doing so, forever changed the course of women's sports in the state of Alabama. It felt right to leave the final words for Noona.

"I believe in girls' athletics," Noona said. "The individuals I coached were athletes who just happened to be girls. I believe that girls are as important as boys. All girls should be given the opportunity to be involved in athletics if they choose. In my life, God directed me to go somewhere others have not gone and to bring about change for the better. By doing so, I pray that I have left a path for others to follow. I hope my efforts were successful. I also believe that the one who rows the boat doesn't have time to rock it. I pray that I did my share of rowing. This is my story."

Chapter 4

Brad Moody

*M*ental toughness is an inner quality that enables a person to stay focused on his or her long-term goals and passions. Brad Moody fits this description that some refer to as plain old grit. Brad is featured here because he captures the essence of grit, having come through adversity in order to live a satisfying and fulfilling life.

"My dad, Robert 'Bob' Moody, set an example for me," said Brad. "He was and still is a remarkable man and supportive father. He set a high standard, and, sometimes, it's a bit daunting to live up to his level of accomplishments. My mom, Frances, is just as outstanding as Dad. She is always supportive, inspiring, and encouraging me in all that I do."

Brad is the youngest of three children, born to Robert and Frances Moody, of Florence, Alabama. His paternal grandparents, Paul and Ollie Moody, who were big influences in his life, lived next door to Brad as he grew up in Florence.

"They loved having us over all the time," said Brad. "One winter, when snow and ice covered the ground, my granddaddy dug a path through the ice and snow in the vacant lot between our houses. This gave us, even when the weather outside was bad, a walkway to visit. They added so much to a happy childhood."

Brad spoke just as fondly about his maternal grandmother, Josephine Jones.

"She worked for thirty years as the head cashier in the business office at ECM Hospital, and she lived on the lake near Tate Slough," Brad said. "She loved having us to the lake for water skiing and boating activities."

Brad's sister, Babs Campbell, is well-known in real estate circles in the Shoals, and his brother, Barry, is Chief of Anesthesiology at ECM.

"I'm immensely proud of my sister and brother," Brad said. "They helped raise me, especially in Auburn, when mom and dad were so busy. We are a close-knit family and love one another dearly, although our busy schedules keep us from visiting often."

The Moody family left Florence in 1966 to live in Auburn, Alabama, when Brad was just three years old. The five years in Auburn created in Brad a dedication to the Big Blue.

"Daddy moved the family to Auburn so he could get his pharmacy degree," said Brad. "He worked a full-time job, helped raise us three children, and attended pharmacy school. He and my always-supportive mom instilled in me a strong work ethic and sound values and principles."

Bob Moody, as was his intention all along, moved the family back to Florence after completing his pharmacy degree in 1971. He set up shop in the old Florence Apothecary building, and thus began Moody Drugs.

"I went to Powell Elementary School, Appleby Junior High School, and graduated from Bradshaw High School," said Brad. "It's strange to realize all three schools no longer exist."

During his years at Bradshaw, Brad developed a love for singing and playing the piano.

"Mom and Dad were charter members of Westminster Presbyterian Church, and we were regulars every Sunday," Brad said. "I sang in the choir, and, despite not being an entertainer, I have a pretty good singing voice. I now confine my singing to my home."

Brad took piano lessons from Rachel Cadenhead and Alan Flowers, both of whom are gifted and noted musicians. Although Brad has a 130-year-old grand piano in his home, he admits that he rarely spends time playing the instrument.

"I could have been good, maybe even accomplished, but I didn't stick with it after college," said Brad, who attended Rhodes College in Memphis, Tennessee. "There were some really talented people there, and it became intimidating. It was a great experience, and I have enjoyed a lifelong love of music. I love all genres, with the exception of rap."

Music wasn't Brad's only interest in high school. He also considered auditioning for the role of the Bradshaw High School mascot, the Bruin, a job that would terrify most students. Like most mascots, The Mighty Bruin was required to wear a suit–in this case, a bear–while performing at sporting events.

"I wasn't too shy, but I didn't try out because I knew the bear suit would be too small," Brad said, with a smile. "Don't tell anyone, but I rescued the bear suit and still have it at home. I don't wear it, at least not often."

After graduating from Bradshaw in 1982, Brad pursued his degree in psychology at Rhodes, which proved to be academically challenging, Brad said, of the small liberal arts college. During Brad's first two years, Rhodes was known as Southwestern at Memphis and had but 900 students enrolled. In 1984, the name was changed to Rhodes College to honor former college president, Peyton Nalle Rhodes.

"I was a tad worried, but my academic skills were strong enough to handle the course study," said Brad. "Initially, I began in pre-med but quickly changed directions into Psychology. I'm a listener and an observer of people. My friends have always referred to me as a caregiver. I seemed to be the person always looking out for others, and I'm still that way now."

Brad completed his degree in psychology in 1986, and he put it to use after graduation when he accepted the position as program manager with Charter Lakeside Hospital in Memphis. At the time, Charter was a premier provider of behavioral health services in the country.

"I loved working for Charter and using my people skills and education from Rhodes," Brad said. "My responsibilities included marketing hospital services to physicians, schools, law enforcement, and the community. I was also responsible for all aspects of the child and adolescent treatment programs. After five years with Charter, to the surprise of my Auburn friends, I enrolled at the University of Alabama to pursue additional education."

Brad secured his Master of Arts in Advertising and Public Relations in 1993 and maintained a 3.63 grade point average while in graduate school. He was admitted into Kappa Tau Alpha, a national journalism and mass communication honor society. After several years back in Memphis, Brad realized that the job, while fulfilling, wasn't his lifelong calling.

"Daddy was running Moody Drugs by himself," said Brad. "I relocated back home in 1995 to assist him in the business. I have lived in Florence since then, and I helped Daddy in all areas and expanded the customer base."

Brad remained with his Dad from 1995 until the store was sold in 2007. Because of their close proximity, Moody Drugs had been friendly competitors with Chad's Payless Pharmacy for many years, so Brad walked inside one day and asked if they needed any assistance. It wasn't long before Brad was hired by Chad's.

"Working for Chad's was similar to what I'd been doing," Brad said. "And I was able to bring many of our former customers over to Chad's. I was busy completing inventory, customer relations, handling special orders, and anything else that was needed."

Brad left Chad's in early 2014 because he felt pulled in a different direction. He was looking for the personal and professional fulfillment he'd experienced early in his career. Brad took a radical and unorthodox step. He signed on as a volunteer at Hospice Advantage.

"I was drawn to the team approach at Hospice Advantage," Brad said. "Surprisingly, it wasn't long before the company offered me a full-time marketing position to educate doctors, nurses, assisted living facilities, and others on end-of-life care. I had been in this role for about eight months when I received a message that the owners of Chad's Payless Pharmacy were interested in having me return to work for them. I accepted their offer and my duties now include marketing the pharmacy to the community."

While it may seem Brad works all the time, he makes time for his special friendships. He is a single man, just turned fifty-two, and loves spending time with friends, although his two best friends live on opposite ends of the United States.

"I've been in love, but, for whatever reasons, marriage hasn't happened," Brad said. "I'm blessed to have many friends, and a few especially dear ones."

One especially close friend, Suzanne Shipper Kushner, from San Francisco, said of Brad, "He is honestly the finest person I know in my life. He's an incredible human being, and it's mostly Brad being Brad."

Brad Moody has accomplished a great deal in his life, and while you seldom hear him complain, he has done so while living with Arnold Chiari Malformation, or ACM, a structural defect in the cerebellum, which is the part of the brain that controls balance.

"I seldom talk about this, but I've had this anomaly since birth," said Brad. "It's affected me with headaches every day of my life. We tried for years and years to get a diagnosis but were unsuccessful. I didn't find out I had ACM until I was thirty-nine, and it was a huge relief finally to know what was causing my symptoms."

ACM is listed as a rare disease and is known to affect less than 200,000 people in the United States. Despite its rarity, there is an effective treatment for ACM.

"You may not believe this, but I referred myself to the Mayo Clinic in Jacksonville, Florida, by making a phone call," Brad said. "My mother rode with me to Florida, and the staff immediately told me they could help. I underwent neurosurgery, and my symptoms are greatly reduced. I'm not cured, but my headaches are now manageable."

Coping with an undiagnosed illness hasn't come to define Brad or his life, so what advice would he offer to others in similar situations?

"Don't give up the search; there is someone out there who can help," Brad said. "Be your own advocate, and control your options. We have highly skilled local physicians, but, in some cases, they may be unable to diagnose rare conditions."

Some turn to the internet, but Brad cautioned against relying on it.

"Be careful about self-diagnosing," Brad said. "The internet is a wonderful tool but can be scary and misleading. My advice is to research facilities, like the Mayo Clinic, that specialize in certain areas."

Life has no guarantees, and Brad's experiences drive that point home. How has grit helped make him the man that he is?

"Everybody faces rejection and tough times in life," Brad said. "I've found that it's best not to take these matters personally. It's difficult, but I never let anything deter me. When situations with people backfire, I still care about the person and tell them so. It's too important. I want to be positive that I've done the right thing. And most importantly, I try to live by these words: Treat people better than you'd like to be treated yourself."

Chapter 5

Mary White Kollefrath

$\mathcal{S}$ome people don't know what they want, but Mary Kollefrath is not one of those
people. She's always wanted to be a wife and a mother. Mary comes by this naturally
because her mom, Carolyn White, also wanted a large family, one that included nine children, but she decided after child number five, who happened to be Mary, that five, rather
than nine, was enough. Mary grew up swimming on the Florence, Alabama, Swim Team
and now directs her passion toward teaching Kate, her granddaughter, along with other
children, how to swim. The highly energetic Mary agreed to sit down with me on a late
Sunday afternoon in the cozy family den that holds so many cherished memories. Ernie,

her husband of thirty-six years, joined us for our visit. Mary is included for the purpose of sharing what she feels is important in life.

Jimmy and Carolyn White, of Florence, made a happy home for their family. Mary's mom, Carolyn, by most accounts, was the youngest person to graduate from the University of North Alabama, formerly Florence Teachers College. She earned her degree when she was but nineteen. Jimmy White, meanwhile, supported the bunch as the owner of Jet Pest Control.

"Mom was the glue that held our family together," said Mary. "She was smart as a whip and could teach any subject. She worked full-time at Jet Pest Control, the family business, but also filled in at Coffee High School whenever her skills were requested. Mama was also a fabulous cook and cared for all five of us kids."

It was Carolyn's White's influence that led Mary to pursue a career in education. After graduating from Coffee High School in 1970, Mary attended and completed her education degree at Jacksonville State University in Jacksonville, Alabama. Mary, a homebody at heart, elected to return to Florence to explore job opportunities.

"Dr. Hot Linville, school superintendent, and friend to Mama, called me saying, 'I have the perfect job for you'," said Mary. "He described the position as being a homebound teacher. The prior teacher had become nervous being in the kids' homes. This didn't bother me one bit, so I accepted the job instantly."

This unique teaching job required Mary to travel throughout Lauderdale County to instruct kids who were dealing with injuries, thus preventing them from attending school. Mary taught kids from kindergarten through 12th grade.

"I was required to teach every subject," said Mary. "I even took Mom with me many times to teach chemistry. I had to be tough regardless of the circumstances, though. It was my job to ensure these students completed their work in order to advance to the next grade."

Mary related one of the many stories she's accumulated after years of teaching students in their homes. She noticed that the father of one of her students had become fond of her during the teaching sessions.

"I was teaching one early afternoon with the man's 9th-grade son," said Mary. "Suddenly, I heard a twang, and the father appeared in the living room with no shirt on playing his guitar. The forty-five-year-old man could have starred in the movie 'Deliverance,' but he kept playing and trying to impress me. Not having a shy bone in my body, I applauded his performance and continued my lesson. He never repeated the audition."

Mary's job changed over the years to include only children who were classified as special-education students. These were the mentally challenged kids and often the ones who had suffered severe head injuries in car accidents.

"I loved my job, even with the emotional aspect of connecting with the kids," said Mary. "I came to love those kids. With them, it was crucial to teach them to make eye contact, to open their hands, and to smile. My goal with them was to get a smile on their faces. It's important to understand that the kids who suffered severe injuries are the same people they were before experiencing the disability. Many of them found new qualities that had not surfaced before. I tried my best to help them cope and adjust to a new normal."

But teaching isn't Mary's only skill. She and her husband, Ernie, had begun a side business out of necessity.

"It was just before the holiday season in 1988 when Ernie's paycheck bounced as high as our Christmas tree," said Mary. "The company he worked for had gone under, and, while I wasn't sure how, I knew I had to make extra money to buy presents for our three young daughters. I was wide awake at midnight, and I began having visions of cheese straws. We had made them for church friends the previous year for Christmas gifts. Everyone loved them, so my mind was envisioning boxes and boxes of cheese straws to solve our money dilemma. This marked the beginning of Mama's Cheese Straws."

The following morning, Mary asked her husband if he would help her in the new endeavor. As the real cook in the family, Ernie's expertise in the kitchen would be sorely needed.

The soft-spoken Ernie said, "I love to cook, and sometimes you can eat what I cook and sometimes you can't. But the folks seemed to like our cheese straws. I would hand crank them out until Mary's brother, Don, bought the Gourmet Shop in downtown Florence. We then invested in a large commercial kitchen to expand the operation."

Initially, this husband-and-wife team intended to make enough money in 1988 to buy some presents for their kids. But the following year, just as the holiday season approached, scores of the Saint Joseph Catholic Church families began calling and requesting Mama's delicious cheese straws.

"Ernie and I couldn't disappoint those wonderful people who bought them the prior year," said Mary. "So we made them again. And we continued making them and began shipping them around the country. We still use the same ingredients that my mom used back in her days. And we are still making Mama's Cheese Straws even today."

Family, including her marriage to Ernie, is the most important thing in Mary Kollefrath's life. She met her future husband on a blind date in 1978, and they were married within the year. They recently celebrated their thirty-sixth wedding anniversary.

"After the first date with Ernie, that was it," said Mary. "We have three incredible daughters and one very spoiled granddaughter."

The Whites offered genuine love and affection to their five children, and it created that trait in Mary, thereby becoming the biggest influence in the way in which she and Ernie raised their girls.

"All five of us adored Mom and her commitment to family," said Mary. "She held everything together on the home front. She passed down her core values and beliefs to us kids. Mom insisted that we occupy the third pew on the right front at First United Methodist Church every Sunday morning, and I do mean every Sunday morning."

Mary's mom and dad are deceased now, and Mary lost her brother, Don, when he was sixty.

"Ernie and I have tried to instill the same values in our daughters as my mom did for us," Mary said. "Material possessions were insignificant to Mom and Dad. We're all about family and relationships. After Mom passed away in 1987, our family settled the estate issues without a cross word being uttered. In fact, if any of my family wanted something the other inherited, the person with the item would give it to them. Don gave me some things, and I returned the favor. I can assure you our daughters feel the same about this issue."

This is a large family, but it's a family that deeply values one another. Not too long ago, Ernie was given six months to live after being diagnosed with cancer. While in some families this could cause discord, for Mary and Ernie, it was further evidence of just how deeply the bonds of family run.

"My three daughters circled the wagons and quickly initiated a game plan," Mary said. "Within two days, we were in Memphis, Tennessee, visiting top specialists in the field. Everything was scheduled by the joint efforts of our girls. The treatments have been difficult but successful, and Ernie is now in remission."

The down-to-earth Ernie joined the conversation.

"The love, support, and hard work provided by my family filled me with gratitude," said Ernie. "Everyone should be so blessed. Family and dear friends didn't give up on me, and the encouragement was humbling."

Mary and her extended family have enjoyed many trips and weekends together, especially attending football games at her beloved Auburn University. However, she caught me by surprise when asked about the most exciting place she had ever visited.

"Without any fear of contradiction, that would be Baptist Memorial Hospital in Memphis, Tennessee," said a smiling Mary. "That is where our first granddaughter was born. Yes, that is the most exciting place ever."

It was becoming obvious that the energetic Mary was getting a bit restless. There were things to do before she returned to Memphis in the morning to teach Kate a few additional swimming strokes. But she offered a few words of wisdom before concluding our visit.

"I have realized, in retrospect, that things would have been fine that Christmas in 1988 if the visions of cheese straws had never entered my mind," said Mary. "I, like most of us, was concerned about giving presents to my children and was missing the point. My incredible Mom, despite being very busy, taught us that you give little when you give possessions, but, if you give your time, then you're really giving. During my brother's illness, we spent time together, especially watching 'Law and Order' every afternoon at four. This was priceless for me and also, I believe, for Don. There is nothing more important than your time, so guard it closely, and give it only to those who deserve and respect it."

Chapter 6

Mike Nale

$\mathcal{M}$ost of us have never experienced the grim and harsh realities of war. But Private 1st Class Mike Nale did just that by serving as a member of the 173rd Airborne Brigade Separate for eight months and seven days in the unforgiving terrain of the Central Highlands in South Vietnam. These deadly battles were brutal, close, and fought in an area filled with vines and thorns, a million leeches, poisonous snakes, and about half of the malaria-carrying mosquitoes in the world. Despite suffering life-altering injuries, this two-time Purple Heart recipient never complained during our late afternoon visit. Mike is featured to remind future generations of the sacrifices made by so many in our armed forces. Mike will also share a few lessons learned from his military combat experience.

Mike is the middle child of three, born to Leon and Dorothy Danley Nale. Mike's two siblings are older brother, Leon Nale Jr., a Navy veteran himself, and sister, Jan Nale Hannah, the emergency room nurse manager at Shoals Hospital in Muscle Shoals, Alabama. Mike's dad, the no-nonsense Leon Nale Sr., was a chief gunner's mate on a torpedo boat during World War II and was attached to the First Marine's Division on Guadalcanal.

"I was a military brat until Dad moved us to Mom's hometown of Florence in 1958," Mike said. "Mom was a stay-at-home mother, and Dad didn't put up with any silliness. If Dad cleared his throat, it meant for us to stop whatever we were doing, and stop we did. I seemed to be the kid always getting into scraps and fights, but I usually came out okay, except for a broken hand at the expense of another kid's face."

Mike attended Gilbert Elementary School, Appleby Junior High, Central High School, and then Coffee High School. He was a self-proclaimed smartass who craved adventure, a craving never quenchable in the classroom. According to Mike, he graduated summa cum laude from the School of Hard Knocks.

"I suppose we grew up hard," he said. "I was always roaming the fields hunting and fishing. I was skilled with firearms by the age of ten, and I knew that school would not be my avenue for success, so I dropped out of high school at seventeen and enlisted in the United States Army."

In 1965, Mike headed to Fort Benning, Georgia, for eight weeks of basic training. After basic, he attended Advanced Individual Training, or AIT, for light weapons infantry at Fort Ord, California, for an additional eight weeks.

"Basic is what you'd expect," said Nale. "The drill sergeants teach you the basics of being a soldier. In AIT, the training becomes more specialized. My training was in light weapons infantry. However, after this training, I volunteered for airborne and was sent to Fort Benning for the three-week crash course. I volunteered because airborne paid an additional fifty-five dollars a month. This increased my pay to one hundred and twenty-three dollars a month. My combat pay in Vietnam was a whopping two hundred and thirty-eight dollars per month."

Jump school was intense, Mike said. The physical training, or PT, was necessary to ensure the soldiers would be ready for the harsh conditions in Vietnam.

After making five jumps, Mike qualified for airborne. He was assigned to Fort Bragg, North Carolina, and the 82nd Airborne Division, Third Battalion, 325th Infantry. During this time, because he was too young to go to Vietnam, Mike received additional training as a combat medic. After almost a year at Fort Bragg, Mike received his orders to go to Vietnam as a member of the 173rd Airborne Brigade Separate.

Also known as Sky Soldiers, this unit was well-known as one of the premier fighting units in the U.S. Army. The average age of the paratroopers who would be engaging the North Vietnamese Army, or NVA, was a mere nineteen. Mike was eighteen when he entered the fray in the dense and snake- infested jungles of South Vietnam in June of 1967.

Mike said, "We fought mostly in the Central Highlands area of South Vietnam. This was the mountainous jungle, and the battles would occur during the monsoon season. We slept on the ground with no protection from the elements. The emerald green deadly Bamboo Vipers were everywhere as were ants, centipedes, rats, leeches, and scorpions. The Bamboo Viper was called the Two Step because of the toxicity of its venom. It's said that a man can take but two steps after being bitten before he is down. Without immediate medical attention, survival is unlikely. Every day you woke up was a good day. Our job was to kill someone, or someone would kill us."

Most soldiers carried between 700 and 1,200 rounds of ammunition for their M-16 rifles. Some carried extra machine gun ammo and extra mortar rounds. Nale also carried twelve to fifteen frag grenades, known to kill anything within a 10-meter radius. Figuring in basic supplies, the average Sky Soldier was conducting missions while burdened with an additional seventy pounds of gear.

How could even basic needs, like sleep, be met?

"We had to man up, and we slept with one finger on the trigger," Nale said. "We soon realized the North Vietnamese Army was a skilled fighting force and far more accustomed to the jungle conditions. We were at a disadvantage being on their home field, but we never backed down from a fight."

Private 1st Class Mike Nale was involved in many deadly firefights against the sophisticated enemy. These battles occurred in the dense jungle, which afforded the soldiers little to no visibility. Enemy troops were often three meters away and were all but invisible. Battles erupted quickly when the NVA fired rounds from their AK-47's, their light machine guns, and their B-40 rockets. The paratroopers returned fire, and casualties mounted during these deadly exchanges.

The Battle of Dak To was among those in which Mike fought. Taking place over the month of November in 1967, it came to be known as one of the hardest fought and bloodiest engagements of the Vietnam War.

Mike recalled a particularly vivid memory of that time.

He said, "Our minds were on alert twenty-four/seven on November 12, 1967, on a clearing operation. Contact was made one-hundred meters after a vicious firefight. The following day, my platoon in Company B was running point on a search-and-destroy mission with two companies in the rear. It was around four in the afternoon on the 13ᵗʰ of November when we made contact. I was the second man from point when we encountered the enemy. After the firing began at four, I was wounded a minute later from the explosion of a B-40 rocket. It exploded a few meters behind me and tossed me airborne. I landed behind a three-foot high termite mound. As crazy as it sounds, this offered me some protection. They had us in the killing zone. It appeared to me the NVA had staged the battle area. Their snipers were firing from their positions atop the bamboo."

Mike continued, "I noticed fellow soldiers killed by sniper fire, and I was certain we would be overrun by the enemy. We were engaged in a battle with NVA regulars. After our men were hit, I heard the moans and screams. Most were yelling for their mom or for God. It was a desperate situation."

It seemed unlikely that Nale would survive this fierce engagement.

"An NVA sniper was firing at me from his position," Nale said. "He was ten feet in the air and camouflaged in the jungle. My own death was looming. My thought was on the military code of 'Die with Honor.' I would not die without inflicting damage on the enemy. I was prepared to take enemy soldiers with me by using my frag grenades. But in an instant that all changed. An angelic music came to me as if God himself were speaking. An unexpected calmness came over me. I knew it was not my day to die."

This furious battle continued throughout the night, and Mike and his comrades lobbed grenades to keep the enemy at bay.

"During the long night, we used grenades, not our M-16 rifles much," said Nale. "This way, the NVA could not locate our position. The fighting became sporadic during the evening. When daylight arrived, I noticed the carnage. There were bodies everywhere. At 8:30 a.m., I felt a tap on my shoulder. I had my bayonet fixed, spun around, and was ready to kill the enemy. But it was three M-60 machine gunners, and they pulled me to safety. Eighteen of thirty-six in our platoon were killed and thirteen wounded, including me. Most were killed by a bullet to the head from sniper fire."

Despite the death and horrific destruction, Mike recalled an event the prior October that allowed for a brief respite from war. He and his comrades were expecting a delicious steak supper.

"Our machine gunners had killed two wild water buffalo," said Nale. "The first one, the young and tender one, was given to the officers in the rear. The one we cooked tasted like shoe leather on your boot. If I hadn't given up, I'd still be chewing on it today. That was my first and last experience of dining on water buffalo."

These lessons came hard and fast to Mike, and, as a teenager, he had to learn quickly.

"Appreciate life each day," said Nale. "Never underestimate anyone. Sometimes, the person you least suspect might be the most dangerous. Tell your friends and family you love them. You never know when the bell tolls for you."

Mike has twice received the Purple Heart for injuries sustained in combat operations. And from comments made by family members, he could have received a family award as well.

"Mike has a heart of gold," said his sister, Jan. "He has always been the family member to show up on special occasions with a card, gift, flowers, or chocolates. He is the best, and I love him dearly."

Upon reflection on his time in a war that proved to be unwinnable, Mike turned briefly philosophic.

He said, "Life is what we make of it sometimes or what we let it make of us."

Nale returned home after the war and spent several years crisscrossing the country, working odd jobs. In 1974, he relocated back home to Florence and began a career as a letter carrier for the United States Postal Service that lasted more than thirty-three years.

Mike beams when discussing his affection for his four adult children and eight grand-kids. He and wife, Phyllis "Lady" Bugg Nale, reside in the beautiful countryside just outside the Florence city limits.

Mike recently celebrated his sixty-sixth birthday, and, despite his age, he accepts his combat injuries without any hint of resentment. He suffers from post-traumatic-stress disorder, or PTSD, a condition that causes him to have horrifying nightmares. Mike was wounded in action three times during his combat tour. Additionally, his health has been affected by exposure to Agent Orange. This chemical defoliant has been found to cause serious health and psychological issues. Despite the health concerns, Mike doesn't complain; instead, he talks fondly about the opportunity to serve his country.

Let's imagine we are soldiers living and fighting in the jungles of South Vietnam. We're facing heat exhaustion, covered in jungle rot, and leeches attach to every part of our bodies. Snakes, rats, spiders, poisonous centipedes, and heavy rain are our daily nemeses. Fire ants, scorpions, and the deadly Bamboo Viper plague us everywhere. Further, the enemy is trying to kill us at every moment.

Mike and his fellow soldiers experienced this daily in jungle warfare during their service in Vietnam.

"It's tough seeing friends killed and body parts on the ground," Mike said. "You never forget this. We suffered from lack of water, little to no food, the elements, and our clothes simply rotted away. Conditions were as miserable as you could possibly imagine."

What does an individual learn from such an experience so early in his life?

"Mindset in crucial," said Mike. "I learned to keep a positive outlook. Many of us veterans have PTSD, a real issue, but one that has a stigma associated with the illness. Put aside your ego, and find help for anything that affects your daily life. And last, but certainly not least, don't ever lose hope. When things appear impossible, there is always hope, and this allows for strength. If I had it to do over, I wouldn't change a thing. I'm proud to have served and honored to be a member of the 173rd Airborne Brigade Separate. We like to say: Once a Sky Soldier, always a Sky Soldier."

Chapter 7

Shirley Williams Self

Shirley Williams Self is a person of deep and unwavering faith. Her life has been centered around her faith, her family, her friends, and, of course, football. Shirley makes it clear that football is fourth on her list, but, without football in her life, she might never have met and married Hal Self, a football player and coach who was also a deeply Christian man. Shirley is certain that God has blessed her enormously during her eighty-six years, and, for that, she said she is eternally grateful. She reflects often on her late husband's wise advice, which was: It's important to be positive and find something beautiful in everything. Shirley is featured to remind us all of important life lessons.

Shirley, the only child of Auburn Porterfield and Iva Mcbride Williams, was born in 1929 in Decatur, Alabama. At the tender age of five, Shirley was stricken by polio, a condition which left her with no feeling in her arms or legs. Fearing a life of disability for their only child, her parents summoned Dr. J.Y. Hamil, a veteran physician who treated many injured and maimed soldiers during World War I.

"It was a blessing Dr. Hamil lived in Decatur," Shirley said. "The treatment he advised was to have my parents move my arms and legs relentlessly over the next five months. He then insisted that Mom get me involved in dancing schools and acrobatics. I began taking tap dancing lessons and acrobatic dance lessons. My life was exercise and more exercise. The treatment worked, and I even won the Shirley Temple dancing award at age seven at the Princess Theater. Exercise has remained a big part of my life, especially tennis. Tennis keeps a person fit and affords the opportunity to forge lifelong friendships. Some of my dearest friendships began on the tennis courts."

Roller skating was another favorite pastime, and she frequently skated through her neighborhood as a child.

"I became skilled in roller skating," Shirley said. "I don't recall falling; instead, I envisioned myself as a young Sonja Henie, the Olympic figure skating champion."

Shirley's mom and her grandparents were active members of Central Baptist Church in Decatur. Her father, however, was raised in the Catholic faith.

"I'm a 'Cradle Baptist'," said Shirley. "I still have the 'Cradle Roll' certificate framed by my mother that is dated September 20, 1932. From my understanding, the mission behind this was for the church to partner with families to ensure the child would be raised according to Christian beliefs."

With the polio scare behind her, Shirley was free to have a normal childhood and adolescence. She played clarinet in the band and was a cheerleader for one year in the eighth grade. Shirley recalled cheering on Friday evenings for a certain football player.

"There were four cheerleaders, and we cheered for the high school games," said Shirley. "I cheered for the quarterback of the Decatur Red Raiders named Harold Self. I had never met Harold, and little did I know that a decade later he would become my husband."

After graduating from high school in 1945, Shirley, at her mom's insistence, attended the now- defunct Gulf Park College for Women, in Gulfport, Mississippi.

"Gulf Park was a two-year school and proved to be a wonderful place to begin my college experience," Shirley said. "I have dear memories and great friends from those days.

After two years, I transferred to Ole Miss in Oxford, Mississippi, to complete my degree in physical education."

But something occurred in Decatur during the summer before Shirley's senior year in college, something that would forever alter her life.

"I fell in love," Shirley said. "My best friend, Bert Timberlake, and I were driving down Second Avenue in the summer of 1948, and when we arrived at Lloyd's Drug Store, I noticed Hal Self – he was now going by Hal – leaning on the rail next to his best friend, Clyde Smith. Hal called me that night and asked me out on a date. I didn't finish my degree, and Hal and I were married in December of 1948. Clyde Smith later told me that Hal said he was going to marry me that day he saw me at Lloyd's."

Not long after saying their I do's, Hal got a visit from Dr. E.B. Norton, who was president at Florence State Teacher's College, now the University of North Alabama. Norton offered Hal the head coaching job in order to restore the university's football team. Hal accepted the offer, and the Selfs moved to Florence in 1949.

The couple came to love Florence and made this their permanent home.

"We had two of our children, Hank and Sue, in the fifties when Hal was working hard coaching football," Shirley said. "At this time, Hal and one assistant, George Weeks, were the only coaches on the entire staff. They did everything."

Shortly after their third child, Gil, arrived, Hal encouraged Shirley to return to school to complete her degree.

"He actually said, 'I think you need something more constructive to do'," Shirley said. "Besides, we needed the money, so I enrolled in Florence State College and obtained my Bachelor of Science Degree in Elementary Education in 1960. I returned to Florence State University in 1970 and secured my master's degree as a reading specialist. I taught school in Florence for the next twenty-nine years. In 1981, Bette Lynne Mardis and I co-wrote a book entitled, 'Steps to Help Your Child Read Better.' Bill Mitchell, President of First National Bank at the time, funded the project, and we were forever grateful. I believe it helped many students."

Teaching quickly became Shirley's passion.

"Teaching was most rewarding," she said. "I taught at Appleby Junior High School, Richards Elementary, and Weeden Elementary School. My specialty was helping those who were slow readers. It touches me when some of my former students, who are now successful adults, tell me about the influence I had in their lives."

Just as Shirley was thriving in her career, so, too, was Hal.

"Hal enjoyed his career immensely," Shirley said. "He worked for Florence State, or UNA, for a total of thirty-three years. Hal's work ethic was astounding, and he was devoted to the University of North Alabama. He received offers from other schools but never wanted to leave this area or the university. Simply put, he loved Florence and UNA."

Just as football was a vital part of their lives, faith, too, was of utmost importance. Shirley and Hal were members of Highland Baptist Church in Florence for fifty-nine years. Shirley sang in the choir and taught Sunday school for over thirty years. However, after Hal was diagnosed with and suffering from Alzheimer's disease, Shirley made the decision to attend and join Trinity Episcopal Church in 2007.

"I love both churches, but I joined Trinity to be with my family," Shirley said. "I have wonderful friends at Highland and Trinity. I had been singing in the Trinity choir until my eyesight began declining about a year ago. I have always loved singing."

Shirley considers herself blessed and lives her life according to one of her favorite scripture verses, Luke 12:48, which reads: "For everyone to whom much is given, from him much will be required."

Shirley is a member of the Rotary Club of Florence, Alabama, the UNA Sportsman's Club, and the P.E.O. Sisterhood, which is an international women's organization with a primary focus on providing educational opportunities for female students worldwide. Shirley also loves attending UNA athletic events. She has also won many local and statewide tennis tournaments. She enjoys travelling, playing bridge, and spending time with her children, grandchildren, and great-grandchildren. She is a member of the Daughters of the American Revolution, or DAR, and was accepted because of a relative on her paternal mother's side of the family.

"William Overton Callis was a Major during the Revolutionary War, and he died in 1814," Shirley said. "He was a soldier, lawyer, patriot, and a delegate of the Virginia convention that ratified the Constitution of Government in the United States in 1788."

Shirley is the proud mother of three children, Hank Self, Sue Self Raines, and Gil Self Sr. She beams with pride when discussing them and her five grandchildren and two great-grandchildren.

"My family blesses me every day of my life," Shirley said. "They are always looking out for my interests. I love them all dearly. Laura Jane, Hank's wife, and Bill Raines, Sue's husband, help me on a weekly basis. They are wonderful."

Other than family, Shirley spoke about some of the friends she has made over the years through her association with tennis.

"We have played senior tennis, super-senior tennis, and super-super-senior tennis after turning fifty," said Shirley. "Jean Holt and Margie Marshall named our group the 'Ole Dears Tournament' in honor of our departed friend, Ann Megar. Etiole Manush, Mary Riley, Rosalie Stevenson, Ferrel Mefford, Martha Parker, Edith Meeks, Donna Ivy, Verna Frey, and Lou Batson, and I met each year in May for lunch and fellowship. We were a team and enjoyed these times of fellowship immensely. I reflect on them with such fond memories."

One memorable day in the life of Shirley took place when the UNA Board of Trustees voted to rename the Flowers Hall Annex the Henry Harold Self Field House. The dedication took place on April 4, 2009.

"Then UNA President Dr. William Cale called me with this news," Shirley said. "It was possibly the most memorable moment of my life. Hal would have been so honored and humbled."

Declining health of our loved ones is one of the toughest times in our lives. In 2007, Hal Self was confined to the Alzheimer's unit at Green Oaks Inn, an assisted living facility. His two good friends, Bill Jones and Hot Linville, were also residents during a portion of Hal's stay.

"Hal was an incredible person," Shirley said. "Even in this condition, his personality kept everyone entertained. He brought joy to the other residents and joy to me. I visited him every day, and Hal insisted that we enjoy our time together. After dinner, Hal would begin singing, I would join in, and the other residents would as well. It's fascinating how music comes back to you. We'd sing 'South of The Border' and our personal favorite, 'I Love You for Sentimental Reasons'."

Even in the hardest of times, Shirley said her husband was always thinking of her and family.

"Hal would conclude the singing by leading us in his favorite church hymn, 'Jesus Loves Me', Shirley said. "All of us in the dining room joined in and sang loudly: 'Jesus loves me, this I know, for the Bible tells me so.' Hal was, without question, the most influential person in my life, and I hold our memories dear."

Shirley celebrated her eighty-fifth birthday on January 11, 2014, by singing a duet with local entertainer Edsel Holden in front of family and friends. It was a special evening.

"Edsel is a dear friend and also a Decatur native," Shirley said. "Edsel discovered that my favorite song was 'I Love You for Sentimental Reasons' because Hal sang it to me till the very end. This special evening reminded me of how God has blessed me in my life. I have always tried to do my best where I am and with what I have. I am and have always been grateful for the strength God has provided me to do little things in a big way. My lifelong mantra can be found in Philippians 4:13. It reads: 'I can do all things through Christ who strengthens me'."

Chapter 8

Lee Freeman

$\mathcal{L}$ee Freeman often spends his days rushing around the second floor of the Florence-Lauderdale Public Library; it's a fitting place for him to work as, throughout his life, he's become something of a walking encyclopedia. On a recent afternoon, Lee has returned to the library after leading a walking tour of downtown Florence that highlights local Civil War history. And already he's involved in another project. The task at hand is his meticulous preparation for an upcoming presentation he will deliver to a Florence civic club on the topic of how best to research one's family heritage. As a self-proclaimed book nerd, it can be spellbinding to hear Lee rattle off facts that relate to these and many other fascinating subjects. Lee is featured here because of his commitment to preserving crucial family history and for sharing his wealth of knowledge with anyone and everyone.

Lee is the eldest of two boys born to William Lee "Bill" Freeman and Mary Lynn Blair Freeman. The Freemans have deep roots in the Florence, Alabama, area. Lee's dad's great-grandfather, Wiley Freeman, lived in east Florence and worked for the Florence Wagon Works Company as a wagon builder. The company was well-known for distributing its wagons across the United States and to many foreign countries.

Lee's great-grandfather, William Joseph Freeman, served as the secretary of the Lauderdale County Singing Association, which was an interdenominational association dedicated to gospel singing, in the early 1900s. William's four sons, Allen, Emory, Vernon, and Earl, followed in their dad's musical footsteps and formed the Burcham Valley Quartet, performing in the 1930s and 1940s.

"They were well-known and played at school dances, churches, and picnics," said Lee. "They were played frequently on the radio, but I cannot find the actual recordings."

It's clear that history has always been important in Lee's life. In addition to what he's learned from his grandfather, Lee's dad, William Freeman, who was a rural letter carrier, instilled a deep sense of honor and integrity into his two sons.

"My parents and grandparents were honest, hard-working people of strong moral character," said Lee. "I've tried to live my life according to the values and principles they taught me. The whole family instilled in me a love of music. While my dad sang in a gospel quartet in the 1980s and performed in local theater, my only musical claim was playing the drums in the Wilson High School band. However, my family instilled in me a deep love for all types of music, including medieval music; secular and sacred, or chant; classical Mozart and Bethhoven; the Dixie Dregs, who fuse jazz, southern rock, and classical; and classic rock, like Jethro Tull."

After high school, Lee attended the University of North Alabama, but he elected to enter the work force just a few credits shy of receiving his degree. His first experience was in the fast-paced restaurant industry until he heard about a job opening at the library.

"I learned a lot working for Frank, owner of Frank's Italian Restaurant, but the frenetic pace of that business was taking its toll on me," Lee said. "I believe God opened a door for me with the role of local historian at the library. God opens doors for all of us, but we must choose to walk inside."

While Lee's brother, William, has been active in the local theater and acting scene, Lee's preference has always been the written word.

"My parents are both avid readers, so I come by this honestly," said Freeman. "Reading is becoming a lost art because of the internet, and so many people have no idea what they are missing. I believe every person should read the Bible. I also recommend people set aside time for some more intellectual study by reading authors such as N.T. Wright. Two of his more intellectual offerings are 'Jesus and the Victory of God' and his 2013 release, 'Paul and the Faithfulness of God,' while two of his more popular books are 'Surprised by Hope' and 'Simply Christian'."

When not home reading for pleasure, Lee can be found at the library helping people explore local history or their family heritage. Many people don't become interested in genealogy until much later in life, but this seems to be changing, according to Freeman.

"Many of the local grade schools are assigning students a genealogy project," he said. "It is satisfying to see these young boys and girls learn about their family members. I assist them, or should I say, their parents, in completing these assignments. I believe it's difficult to truly know who you are if you don't know where you've been. You will be fascinated by what you discover, both good and bad."

Lee spoke briefly about how one might best undertake the job of researching his family lineage.

"I tell everyone to start with the known and work toward the unknown," said Freeman. "This is a process that requires documentation. My recommendation is to begin at home by looking for marriage licenses, family Bibles, and old photos. Search for funeral programs, obituaries, and interview all living relatives. Swap information with cousins and other relatives. You will be pleasantly surprised how much information is available in the home. Almost every organization like Daughters of the American Revolution, or DAR, requires proof through written documents to certify accuracy."

Locating valuable information on family history can also be performed through an internet search.

"Every county in every state has a United States GenWeb page," Lee said. "The individual who coordinates the Lauderdale and Colbert county sites is local genealogist Pat M. Mahan. The web address for her Lauderdale page is: http://www.rootsweb.ancestry.com. It is linked to pages for all of the surrounding counties. This is one incredible resource, and it's free to the public."

Further, Lee said that many people contact him at work regarding their relatives' final resting places. Lee is a member of the Lauderdale County Cemetery Rehabilitation Authority, or LCCRA, which is sponsored by the Lauderdale County Commissioners, and whose job it is to document, map, and preserve the 430 cemeteries in Lauderdale County. Founded through the efforts of local historian Billy Sledge, the group is led by Dr. George Makowski, a history and political science professor at the University of North Alabama.

"We are presently inventorying and documenting the 430 cemeteries in Lauderdale County," Lee said. "This is a team effort, and we are committed to documenting and preserving every known cemetery in Lauderdale County."

For the past two years, Lee has led a tour with the help of colleagues for the Florence-Lauderdale Public Library called the Footsteps of the Blue and Gray Civil War Tour. It highlights areas in downtown Florence that have a connection to the Civil War. The Florence Masonic Temple, for instance, was accidently burned by Union soldiers when they set fire to several downtown businesses, among them a nearby blacksmith shop, which was making artillery wheels for the Confederate effort.

"Many Union soldiers were also Masons and may have believed their bond as Masons superseded their allegiance to the North or the South," Lee said. "In many cases, Union officers would be reluctant to burn a Confederate Lodge because of this Masonic fraternity."

In addition to local history, Lee is involved with the Alabama Renaissance Faire. During his twenty-five-year tenure, he's served as a board member of the Round Table, the all-volunteer, non-profit group led by founder and chairman Billy Warren. This is this group that plans the local faire. The month of October in Florence, Alabama, has been designated Renaissance Month. There are Medieval-era and Renaissance-era lectures, concerts, and costume-making workshops; the third Saturday is designated for the Royal Autumn Feaste that takes place in the Florence-Lauderdale Coliseum.

"The Renaissance Faire was begun as a way to tie in history with education and the arts," said Freeman. "The event founders felt this could be a type of living history. We cover the life and times of the Medieval and Renaissance periods of history, but we encourage an emphasis on the Renaissance between 1350 AD and 1530 AD. You will see belly dancers, bakers, and blacksmiths plying their trades. The King and Queen preside over the feast, and medieval entertainment is featured. This is something everyone should try at least once."

One might assume that a person engaged in this activity would be outgoing and have little to no inhibitions. But Lee Freeman, who now speaks confidently in front of large gatherings of people, said this was not always the case.

"I was such an introvert in high school that it terrified me to get up and speak in front of the class," said Lee. "It's been a gradual process of confronting my fears and developing the confidence necessary for public speaking."

What advice would Lee offer those who are terrified of speaking in public?

"I wish there was a magic pill because I would have been the first to take it," said Lee. "All of our lives are filled with anxiety, but I believe we must confront any fears in order to enjoy a truly fulfilling life. It's easy to withdraw from things that make us uncomfortable, but, in doing so, one misses out on so much in life. If I can do it, anybody can. In fact, I now worry about overcompensating for my shyness in the old days. Some friends will now say, 'Lee, your feelings are noted, but we've heard enough from you.' I plead guilty to talking too much when my favorite subjects are on the agenda."

Let's imagine for a moment that you are living in the Shoals during the Civil War-era of the 1860s. You are the minister of First Presbyterian Church, Florence's oldest Christian congregation, founded, like the town itself, in 1818. On this Sunday morning, July 27, 1862, you've completed the part of the Presbyterian liturgy that offers prayers for the President and the government, which, in this case, happens to be Jefferson Davis and the Confederate States of America.

Before you are able to make the short walk to your home on Court Street, you are escorted from the pulpit and placed under arrest by future Supreme Court Justice, Union Provost John Marshall Harlan, of the 10th Kentucky Regiment, USA, who, along with some of his men, is attending divine services in your congregation. They have arrested you based on a recent order issued by General Ulysses S. Grant that any Southerner who offers public support for the Confederate States Government is to be arrested on charges of treason and sedition.

The Rev. Dr. William Mitchell experienced this scenario and was a prisoner of war at the Union Prisoner of War Camp in Alton, Illinois, for six months. Fortunately, the Rev. Dr. Mitchell, unlike many other prisoners, survived the ordeal.

If you decide to slow down and take time to listen, there is nobody more qualified than Lee Freeman to let you feel the deep pain and loss experienced by our local ancestors, including the Rev. Dr. Mitchell.

"I would love to have everyone join me on our tour, but don't wait on me," said Lee. "Take your own walking tour around your downtown area and learn about the special places and the people who contributed to the town in which you live. You might even stumble upon some family history that will change your life in a positive manner. If you are a bit nervous, or unsure about how to start, you can always come by and see us at the Florence-Lauderdale Public Library."

Chapter 9

Evie VanSant Mauldin

S ome people search for meaning in all the wrong places and run far too many unim-portant races. Evie VanSant Mauldin is not one of them. She learned early on what she believed constituted a successful and fulfilling life experience. This lesson was further instilled in Mauldin when she was a college student at the University of Alabama. Evie feels that our time here is meant to be shared with the people who respect and embrace us as genuine friends. In her case, this includes her immediate family, especially her sisters, Martha and Mary Marshall, and her many trusted friends. Evie is featured to remind us about what truly matters in the grand scheme of things.

Evie grew up in North Florence as the eldest daughter of three girls to George and Betty Jo VanSant. Her early childhood memories are of playing games with the neighborhood kids in one of the family's large backyards. These were the good ol' days when kids played outdoors until moms called them in at dark or dinner, whichever came first.

"We had a neighborhood club called Scrawny Squirrels," said Evie. "Mary White and Colby Stockard were the leaders, and we kids were the minions. Our uniforms were Liberty Supermarket brown grocery sacks that we turned upside down with our heads sticking out of holes we cut. Mary lined us up in a horizontal line, and we awaited her command. She would call out a name and ask that girl to step forward in front of the group. We were told to yell our name, sing a song of their request, and be scrutinized by Colby and Mary's unrelenting criticism. I suppose they were fun days."

Evie's tough and athletic father, George VanSant, ran the Hurston family farm in Tuscumbia, Alabama, and he insisted his daughters learn the business. He instructed them on how to drive a tractor, care for the horses, take the boat to the river, and back the trailer down the boat launch. There were always chores to be done on the farm that has been in the family for seven generations.

"Dad always wanted a son, so he treated us exactly like the boy he never had," said Evie. "He taught us to be self-reliant. My sisters and I learned to ride horses by sitting in front of our parents on an English saddle. By the age of eight, we were riding by ourselves. My sisters, Martha Zuelke and Mary Marshall VanSant, and I have all become accomplished riders."

Evie's maternal grandmother, Evelyn Hurston, for whom Evie is named, was living on the family farm when Evie was a child. Grandmother Hurston felt that she was missing the party, so the sixty-year-old decided she'd do something about it.

"Grandmother went to Lillian Cook-Deibert and took horseback riding lessons," said Evie. "She learned how to ride and bought a horse named Prince from the Deiberts. She was soon accompanying us on our special weekend adventures. It takes nerve to begin riding at sixty, and she had it. Grandmother came to love the afternoons of riding the trails with us on the farm. Mom and Dad joined us on these family outings."

Evie attended Gilbert Elementary School, Appleby Junior High, and Coffee High School. While attending Coffee, she often felt humiliated when her Dad would drop her off at school in his pick-up with his dogs in the bed, barking at fellow students.

"Can you imagine this as a high school freshman?" said Evie. "Oh, I now drive a pick-up, and my dog rides everywhere with me. My father also refused to allow us to watch TV as kids, and I felt at the time this was cruel and unusual punishment. But upon reflection, it was the best decision. Dad insisted we learn something useful that would help us down the road. I feel blessed to have such caring and supportive parents."

For Evie Mauldin, this "something useful" is outdoor activities, including golf, tennis, and boating.

She excelled as a student and knew in the eleventh grade she wanted to become a lawyer. Evie gained legal experience during the summer between her junior and senior years by working as an unpaid intern for the law firm of Poellnitz, Cox, McBurney, Robinson, and Jones in Florence.

"All of these men were smart, but there was something special about Mr. Charles Poellnitz," said Evie. "He was so scholarly and such a gentlemanly person. This experience instilled in me a passion to pursue a legal career. I doubted my abilities, but my Grandmother VanSant kept insisting how smart I was. I suppose I came to believe her. She was a special influence in my life."

It is clear, even in passing, how important family is to Evie. Many families lack the same camaraderie that she enjoys, so is there some magic to unlocking the secret behind strong familial bonds? Does she anticipate future problems when the family farm will be passed to the next generation?

"None," she said emphatically. "I would give my two sisters everything I have in a minute if they were in trouble. I am positive they feel the same."

Relationships, and not just those with her family, are of utmost importance in Evie's life. What makes her relationships work?

"Spend time with the right people," she said. "If negative people are your friends, then you might consider embracing new friends. Some people refuse to dismiss unhealthy relationships. You and you alone are responsible for your happiness."

While she and husband Fennel have no children of their own, Evie said she's learned that young women need the kind of guidance with which she and her sisters were raised.

"I'd encourage them to be self-reliant, to make their own way in the world," said Mauldin. "You must create the life you desire. If you find a great partner, then your personal journey becomes far more enriching. Never allow fear to interfere with your dreams."

This is a guiding principle in Evie's life. When she transferred to Alabama after two years at a women's college, she quickly developed friendships that have withstood the tests of time and distance.

"Eight other women had transferred, and we became sorority sisters," said Mauldin. "We developed a close bond while living on the same floor in the sorority house. After taking a trip together to Gulf Shores, Alabama, in college, we named ourselves the Big Nine. Ever since college, we have taken one trip a year and have remained lifelong friends. We have each other's backs at all times."

After completing her law degree from the University of Alabama, Evie returned to Florence and was hired by Bank Independent as its only attorney. Today, she's been with the bank for thirty-four years and is the senior vice president and general counsel.

"I cannot imagine doing anything else," beamed Mauldin. "Most of my duties are overseeing real estate transactions by the bank. I'm responsible for overseeing all documents used for commercial loans in the bank. The job requires problem-solving skills, and I used those to convince the bank to hire Missy Ridgeway more than seven years ago as the second attorney in the bank. I'm also involved with our branch locations to assist with and answer any legal questions that arise. We stay busy."

Mauldin's passion away from the office is the exhilarating sport of fox hunting. She holds the distinction as a Master of Fox Hounds, one of four Masters for the Mooreland Hunt, a group founded in the early 1960s by Harry Moore Rhett Jr., a prominent community leader in Huntsville, Alabama. This is a mid-sized hunt, with sixty or so members, and it has become one of the most highly respected in North America.

Evie also serves as the first flight Field Master. This is the person who leads the group of mounted, unarmed fox-hunters, who closely follow the foxhounds as they chase coyotes and foxes for as many as twenty miles on any given day. This sport is not for the faint of heart, and one must be a skilled horseman in order to consider participation.

"I love fox hunting," said a beaming Mauldin. "This is not shooting; this is hunting. That is a distinction that was originally made in England, where the sport of fox hunting began. When you go shooting, you go out with a gun; when you go hunting, you go on horseback and follow the hounds. They are the ones doing all of the work."

Hunting requires a great deal of athletic skill, and not just from the hunters.

"The hounds have been bred to hunt, and they are highly trained athletes," Evie said. "Because hounds are pack animals, they work as a team, and it's fascinating to watch each hound develop his or her unique skill. We like to say that fox hunting is not just a way of life – it is a life. And it's a life that I get to share with my best friends, my sisters as well as my two nieces. After the hunt, we begin the tailgate. This isn't your football tailgate with motor homes, because we just lower the gate on the pick-up. That's our tailgate. And our stories are better than old high school football tales. Ours are truthful – well, almost."

Blessed to share her passion of fox hunting with her family and friends, Mauldin also spoke about the importance of staying in touch with dear friends from school days.

"What's more important than family and friends?" said Mauldin. "Life is unsatisfying and meaningless unless shared with our close friends and family. I cannot imagine refusing to make time for family and friends. It's too important."

While most of us struggle with how to spend our free time, the Big Nine have one weekend per year reserved for fellowship and fun. This weekend is restricted to others, as it's reserved only for the nine members, no husbands or partners allowed. In fact, a few letters had to be written to husbands to advise them that no more membership applications would be considered.

"Every trip since college has been special," Evie said. "But one stands out because of the location of a baby shower. We decided to celebrate one member's baby shower at the Pink Pony Pub on the beach in Gulf Shores, Alabama. Each member wore a sleeveless t-shirt with the words Pink Pony emblazoned on it. We were nine best friends sharing a priceless moment twenty years ago in a unique and special place."

Each member of the Big Nine is now approaching her sixtieth birthday, and life has dealt everyone their playing cards. During many emotionally trying times, however, each member has always supported the other eight unconditionally.

"The hard times in life have surfaced," said Evie. "We've experienced parents' deaths, children's deaths, siblings' deaths, and other painful issues. Job loss, divorce, financial problems, and personal health issues have demanded our attention. But through it all, good and bad, one thing has remained set in stone. Not one of the Big Nine has failed to offer crucial support to the others when needed. To know friends are there for you, no matter what, is a feeling that defies words. I pray that everyone makes time to develop this type of unconditional love for their dearest friends.

An honest answer is the sign of a good friend and true friendship never ends. I believe this with my heart and soul, and I feel blessed to have such caring and compassionate friends Lastly, you may regret how you spent some of your time, but I don't believe you'll regret times spent with those you love and respect."

Chapter 10

Danny Hendrix

he Lauderdale County Revenue Commissioner stands an inch or two above fight feet in height, but don't for a minute allow his diminutive stature to fool you. Danny Hendrix is a man of action and vast accomplishments and is unwilling to rest on his laurels. Some have said that being small in stature hinders a person's ability to achieve things in life. Danny has been defying this misconception throughout his life thanks to his many accomplishments in the sports arena and the classroom. Danny is included here because he defies those stereotypes in a way few others can.

It is a bit shocking to see, in person, the sheer small size of the man that is Danny Hendrix. His body weight seldom fluctuates and remains approximately one hundred and twenty-eight pounds. Part of the reason could be that, before entering politics, Danny owned and operated Ron's Gym in Florence, Alabama.

"I began working out at Ron's Gym in 1974 and purchased the business in 1989," said Danny. "It was my livelihood from 1989 until I sold it in 2001. I continued working out there until the new owner went out of business in 2005. I've been exercising since then at the YMCA. Exercise is vital to maintaining good health, and everyone should get involved. You're welcome to join me late afternoons at the Y. I'll take it easy on you at the beginning."

Danny is the eldest of three boys to Tom and Jean Hendrix. His father was a natural athlete and a four-sport letterman in Tuscumbia, Alabama. His dad is widely-known for Tom's Wall, an incredible engineering feat he constructed of stones for the purpose of honoring his great-great-grandmother. The wall is located in front of Tom's home, just east of the Natchez Trace Parkway at milepost 338 in Northwest Alabama.

"I built the wall to honor Te-lah-nay," said Tom Hendrix. "She was removed, along with thousands of others, at the age of seventeen in the Trail of Tears relocation of the Native Americans in the early 1800s. She later escaped from the Oklahoma reservation and endured a five-year journey, on foot, back to this location. It has taken me thirty-five years to complete my tribute, and it's been fulfilling beyond words. My project is the largest unmortared wall in the United States."

There's no question that Danny's proud of his dad's remarkable accomplishment.

"The wall is a marvel, without question, and it has brought national attention to the area," said Danny. "One elder of the Yuchi Indian tribe said to Dad, 'All things shall pass. Only the stones will remain.' The wall contains stones from over 120 countries that come in every size, shape, and texture you can imagine. The wall belongs to the people, and everyone is welcome. Dad might give you a personal tour."

The wall came later in Danny's life. Before it, he had to work through other family issues.

"My mom and dad divorced when I was in the sixth grade," he said. "I was first living with mom but made a hard decision to move in with Dad just before entering the ninth grade. It turned out to be the right decision for me."

It was during this transition that Danny joined the Florence Swim Team at the Royal Avenue swimming pool. He quickly added another water skill to his resume.

"The diving came easy to me," he said. "Jimmy Stanfield was director and coach of the team, but fellow diver Marcia Wiggin was instrumental in helping me on diving technique. Her influence was crucial to my success."

Danny became accomplished on the one-meter and three-meter diving boards. The muscular little man claimed second-place in the state for three consecutive years in the late 1960s in the diving competition. This was not as part of a high school team but events associated with swimming clubs throughout the state of Alabama.

Danny's diving exploits were not always related to competition, either. While in high school, he once climbed to the top of Shoal Creek Bridge and performed a special dive.

"Don't tell anyone because I could be arrested," Danny said. "But I did climb to the top of the bridge, a height of approximately thirty-five feet from the surface of the water, and I completed a one- and-a-half summersault tuck into the creek. Those were the good old days."

Long past those glory days of diving, it's easy to assume that chapter of his life is closed. But that's not the case, according to Danny.

"Last year, I travelled to Point Mallard in Decatur, Alabama, for an afternoon of diving," said Danny. "I easily nailed a back one-and-a-half with a twist off the three-meter board. I considered this to be my fifty-eighth birthday present to myself. It had been ten years since I had been on a three-meter board. It actually came back to me quite easily."

While diving remains a fun hobby, Danny has taken on another role, one that required him to win an election.

"I didn't have a political bone in my body until Mickey Haddock suggested I consider running for office," Danny said. "This was around 1996, and I was also encouraged by my uncle, Grady Liles. I heeded their advice and have never regretted my decision."

These days, most of Danny's time is spent overseeing a staff of twenty-one employees as the Lauderdale County Revenue Commissioner. Despite such responsibility, Danny seemed relaxed on one hectic Wednesday morning.

"I really enjoy my job, even with the stressful days," he said. "The secret is to work hard and make certain everyone is accountable for their job duties. I am also blessed to have a responsible and devoted group of employees."

How would he classify his management style?

He said, "My motto is: 'Let's get it done.' My business philosophy is results-oriented. We function as a team and pull together for positive results. Our main goal is to ensure that all Lauderdale County property owners understand their property tax implications. Our office is responsible for the assessment of both real, including land and buildings, and business personal property such as furniture, machinery, and equipment for all of Lauderdale County."

Athletics, especially those he played in high school, have taken on a crucial role in shaping the person that is Danny Hendrix, including the management style he brings to his current role.

"That is so correct," said Danny. "I decided to give wrestling a go when they requested volunteers in the ninth grade. I was immediately taken in by the individual aspect of the sport. Team sports are great, but, in wrestling, there is no one to blame but yourself. The lesson is accountability. You and you alone control your destiny. I'm still upset about letting that opponent pin me in the tenth grade."

Danny learned his lesson well. He finished third in the state as a junior, and he claimed the state title his senior year. Danny was also named an Honorable Mention All-American wrestler his senior year in 1973.

"Preparation is the key to success," he said. "This is true for anything in life. I was so well prepared my senior year in 1973 to win that state title."

Danny was more than ready to begin his college years at Florence State University. He excelled in the classroom and as a cheerleader for the Lions. Cheerleading was a natural fit for Danny as it combined the strength he gained as a wrestler and the lean muscles he honed as a swimmer and diver. Besides, wrestling and diving weren't options for student athletes then a FSU. During Danny's tenure at FSU in 1974, Florence State changed its name to the University of North Alabama, symbolizing its coming of age as a comprehensive, regional university.

"Many people don't realize the time demands on a cheerleader," he said. "I was on the squad my sophomore through my senior years and was head cheerleader my last year. One of my fondest memories was cheering in front of a full house at Flowers Hall during our basketball team's run to the Gulf South Conference Championship. Coach Bill Jones and his Lions finished this magical season with a third place finish in the 1977 NCAA Men's Division II Basketball Tournament in Springfield, Massachusetts."

There's more to Hendrix than athletics, however. He is a charter member of the Alpha Tau Omega fraternity at UNA and served the organization as treasurer for two years. In 1977, Danny assumed the responsibility as president of the Interfraternity Council. He was also named Mr. UNA his senior year on campus. Despite these accomplishments, Hendrix remains a humble individual.

"I'm not one to toot my own horn," he said. "The scripture is clear: All men are created equal. God has blessed each of us with certain gifts. It is our responsibility to use them wisely and for God's intended purpose."

Despite not being raised in church, Danny is a man of deep faith. He is a family man who loves activities with his wife, Deborah, and son, Jay. Danny and his family are now active members of College View Church of Christ.

"We, as a society, have become too darn serious," he said. "Work is important, but it is okay to have a laugh or two. Work hard, take care of business, but enjoy the ride. Most importantly, don't take yourself too seriously, because no one else does. I find something to laugh about every day of my life."

Despite the challenges he's faced, Danny has a positive outlook on life.

"Everyone will experience setbacks," said Danny. "The key to a fulfilling life is how you deal with these issues. Get outside in nature because this allows for clarity to focus on what's important in life. Go for a long walk or jog in our local parks. But most importantly, keep your issues in their proper perspective."

Danny has learned over time that it's okay, to solicit advice from others.

"We men can be reluctant to ask for help," he said. "Many of us consider this a weakness. It's perfectly okay to call someone for help. And remember: God is always there to listen. Don't allow anyone to make you feel uncomfortable in your personal relationship with God."

Danny Hendrix is a remarkable combination of size and strength, not just physical but a deep and undeniable spiritual strength. Being around him even briefly brings out the need to smile. And, true to form, he celebrated his sixtieth birthday with a splash and some diving at Point Mallard.

It is clear age doesn't stand a chance against Danny and his dynamic spirit. Already, he's making plans for 2017 and an afternoon of fun on the water.

"Mark your calendar for July 7, 2017, for a little celebration at Shoal Creek," he said. "Don't tell the authorities, but I might re-enact my one-and-a-half summersault tuck off of the Shoal Creek Bridge. Come join me, and, if we don't dive, we'll enjoy an afternoon of water skiing."

Chapter 11

Cassandra Scott Allen

$\mathcal{C}$assandra Scott Allen wears a smile when making her rounds as a licensed practical nurse at Merrill Gardens assisted living facility in Florence, Alabama. She speaks animatedly about being one of the first employees hired sixteen years ago when the facility first opened to the public. In fact, Cassandra was there when the carpet installers were putting the finishing touches on this new home for senior citizens. As our loved ones embrace the final journey of their lives, it is Cassandra and others like her who work to ensure they maintain their dignity and respect. Cassandra is featured to let everyone know about the crucial role played by nurses during this time in the lives of the residents and the family members.

"In most cases, this is their last stop," said Cassandra. "I feel an obligation to the residents to make them as happy as possible during this stage of life. It's an emotional time for the residents, their family members, but also for us, the employees. I have come to love these men and women."

Cassandra is the youngest of three children of career Marine father James Scott and working mom Mary Scott. While her father was away on job assignments, her mom was the glue that held the family together. After graduating from Coffee High School, Cassandra attended Samford University in Birmingham in the spring of 1989 with plans to pursue a career in education. However, when she was home for the winter of 1991, her plans were sidetracked when she met the man she would marry.

"I met and married Marcus Allen, not the famous football player, and I returned to college after Christmas break, but I ended up coming back home after just two months," she said.

During this time, Cassandra worked at Rogers Department Store in downtown Florence and then at the front desk at Colonial Manor Hospital, what is now Eliza Coffee Memorial East, on Cloyd Boulevard in Florence.

"This was before my calling to become a nurse," Cassandra said. "Marcus and I recently celebrated our twenty-second wedding anniversary, despite the fact that we attended rival high schools in Florence. Marcus is a Bradshaw Bruin, and I'm a Coffee High School Yellow Jacket, and we now cheer for Florence High School, and, of course, Central High School, the county school attended by our two sons."

The friendly and unassuming Allen shared a difficult and life-changing moment when her mother, Mary Scott, matriarch of the family, fell ill on a trip to Atlanta. Everyone rushed to Cobb County Hospital where Mary was being treated for a severe brain hemorrhage. Despite outstanding care by the doctors and nurses, Mary passed away at the relatively young age of forty-nine.

"It was at that moment I knew my career would change directions," Cassandra said. "I experienced a calling to be a nurse. I wanted to know everything possible about helping others in these situations. Mom was my best friend, and I felt maybe if trained properly, I could have done something to help. I know now there was nothing anyone could have done."

Cassandra abandoned her education plans and began working at Merrill Gardens in 1999 as a resident assistant. While at Merrill, she attended nursing school at Northwest-Shoals Community College and obtained her Licensed Practical Nurse Certificate in 2001.

"I have been here at Merrill since the beginning in 1999," Cassandra said. "I have observed how everything has come together to provide a loving and supportive home for the residents. We opened with just one gentleman in the facility but filled up quickly in about six months. Merrill now has sixty-eight apartments and all are filled at this time. We have studio, one-bedroom, and two-bedroom apartments. There are several couples who live with us at this time. Our resident count at present is seventy-four."

This assisted living facility offers assistance to residents in many ways depending on their specific needs.

"We offer what we refer to as activities of daily living," Cassandra said. "The resident pays an additional fee for these services which include help in showering, getting dressed, and other activities. While the job can be tedious, physically demanding, and emotionally draining, it also provides deep satisfaction and fulfillment. I find enormous joy and happiness in caring for and getting to know our residents. Most show their appreciation for our efforts. I wouldn't change a thing."

Cassandra spoke of experiencing a deep spirit of camaraderie among her fellow employees. All of them work together for the common purpose of providing the best available care for the residents.

"One of the best parts of my job is having fellow employees to lean on for support during those hard days," Cassandra said. "We deal with tough issues and concerns in this business. I cannot imagine working somewhere if the employees are pulling in opposing directions. We're a team, and the team goal is to help maximize function and quality of life for our residents."

I was curious about the foundation of this person who always seems to display such an upbeat and friendly demeanor.

"The two major influences in my life were my mom and my dear maternal grandmother," said Cassandra. "While mom has been gone many years, Mae Cole is alive and well at the age of eighty-six. My grandmother, Mae, lived across the street from us growing up, and she is an incredible woman of deep faith. She and Mom raised us in Rock Primitive Baptist Church, a small country house of worship with around two hundred members. My husband and I are members of Christ Chapel Church but still love visiting Rock Primitive with my grandmother."

I could sense the deep emotional love in Cassandra when discussing her late mom and her grandmother. Her eyes revealed the enormous impact and unconditional support and love offered by these two women. But life, with its ups and downs, was not finished with this family. In 2003, Cassandra's brother and nephew were killed in an automobile accident.

"I knew it was my time to step forward and offer support for the family," said Cassandra. "Grandma had told me nothing in life was as difficult as losing a child. Now, she was faced with the death of a grandchild and a great-grandchild. But Mae Cole, once again, comforted every person in our extended family. She does so with her deep and unyielding faith in God."

With a few tears rolling down her face, Cassandra said, "When faced with the most difficult life issues, I always think to myself, 'What would Grandma want me to do?' This will be with me forever. She is truly one incredible person of deep and uncompromising faith."

Cassandra's smile widens when speaking about her two children, sons Andrew and Jeremiah. Both are football players, and the entire family attends these special Friday night games. The joy and pride revealed by a normally reserved Cassandra spoke volumes about the family connections that are strengthened by sharing these once-in-a-lifetime moments. Her oldest son, Andrew, has graduated from Central High School and decided to serve his country by enlisting in the United States Air Force in April of 2015. Jeremiah is a sophomore at Central and should provide a few more Friday night football memories for the extended family.

I couldn't help but wonder how Cassandra maintained that smile, despite such a demanding schedule.

"I always find something to laugh about," she said. "There is something going on in everyone's life that can produce a chuckle. This is important in all of our lives. We laugh about something every day at work. It relieves stress and makes life more enjoyable."

The soft-spoken yet confident Cassandra Allen seemingly has the important life issues in proper perspective. She is keenly observant and always looking to offer assistance to a resident in distress. I sensed that she might be withholding valuable information to help us all.

Cassandra said, "I know that every one of us is fighting some battle every day. We are pulled in many different directions by our jobs and family responsibilities. But, in my life, I've discovered it's the residents who make me happy. Despite suffering from many age-related issues, most of them remain upbeat and positive. They are my inspiration. It's my duty to give them something to smile and laugh about every single day."

I couldn't help asking if Cassandra had a favorite person from her sixteen years of caring for so many people. Her eyes revealed a positive response.

"Why, yes, I do, but I will never tell," said Cassandra. "These special bonds will forever remain between me and the family. But I have come to love all of our former and present residents."

What advice might she offer to someone considering a career in nursing?

"Being a good nurse requires a special kind of person, an individual who really cares," Cassandra said. "It's not a glamorous job, and it requires many skills that cannot be taught in the classroom. For example, no professor can teach you how to cry with a patient when he or she receives a devastating report from the doctor. The classroom is unable to teach you how to find dignity when giving a patient a bed bath. Search inside yourself, and you'll know if this career fits your personality. If it does, you'll discover enormous satisfaction despite the many challenges of the profession."

An average day in the workplace gives a hint at some of the challenges presented in nursing.

"Our main job is to assist," Cassandra said. "We help the residents in all areas of their lives. We monitor their medications and closely watch for any acute issues that might require physician intervention. Our job is a collaborative effort among us, the resident, and the family members, with the mutual goal of helping the patient enjoy a more active and fulfilling life. Another satisfying part of my job is getting to know the family members who visit frequently. I've developed good friends over the years as a result of these interactions."

As our time was slowly coming to an end, it seemed clear that Cassandra has never regretted the career change she made after seeing her mom in the hospital following a massive stroke.

"That is for certain," said Cassandra. "I love my career as a nurse and wouldn't change a thing. Some things happen for a reason. Because of mom's untimely death, my calling to become a nurse changed my life forever. Mom was my dearest friend, and I hope she would be proud of me. I think she would."

Cassandra was overcome by emotions when reflecting on her mom and the many patients she has assisted during her sixteen-year nursing career. It seemed fitting to leave the final words to her.

"Being a nurse is a heart-and-soul experience," said Cassandra. "I do the best I can to care for and give a hug, touch of the hand, nurture, teach, or just listen to the residents. Nursing is a physically and emotionally exhausting profession, but it also affords me the privilege of working with fascinating people from all walks of life.

"We often see people at their worst, and we are there during the most intimate, challenging, and frightening moments in their lives. We are by their side. It's about being able to love people when they are at their weakest moments and make a difference in their lives on a daily basis. Nursing is not for everyone, but it sure is for me."

Bart Black

*W*isdom is the ability to think and act using knowledge, experience, common sense, and insight with good intentions. This involves an understanding of people, things, situations, and the ability to apply judgment before engaging in a certain course of action. Bart will be the first to tell you that he has not always exercised good judgment. In fact, he learned a valuable lesson several years ago in regards to actions and behaviors in front of children. Bart Black is included in order to share this lesson and a few more learned from the most influential person in his life, his dad, Clyde "Sappo" Black.

Bart was born the middle child to Clyde C. "Sappo" Black and Sandra Lee Black, of Jasper, Alabama.

"Dad was a Korean War veteran and one incredible father," said Bart. "His lifelong best friend was George Lindsey of 'The Andy Griffith Show.' Because of dad's friendship with George, we were fortunate to know people like Buck Trent and Roy Clark from the country music scene. Buck, who invented the electric banjo, picked out my first guitar when we visited him in Nashville in 1974. I learned about humility from Dad and his accomplished but down-to-earth friends."

It is impossible to dismiss the admiration and respect Bart has for his late father. Bart and his father were both graduates of the University of North Alabama. His dad returned to Jasper after his graduation and lived the rest of his life in Walker County.

"My dad never missed a sporting event I played," said Bart. "He also taught me the art of fly fishing and hunting. My brother, Gregg Black, and sister, Cindy Black McDonald, and I all attended UNA because of dad's influence. Ironically, Gregg, the youngest, was the first to graduate. It took me sixteen years to finish, but I did graduate on the Dean's List. Cindy, the smartest among us three, took even longer to get her degree. I finished a year ahead of Cindy in 1995."

Bart's family is still involved with UNA through the Clyde "Sappo" Black award given during the annual George Lindsey Film Festival.

"Dad and George were compassionate individuals who gave freely of their time to help others," Bart said. "Both have passed away, but their legacy lives on at the University of North Alabama."

Bart has been self-employed as a businessman for many years in the Shoals. He first owned Parkway Pak-N-Ship and is now involved in real estate development. His intoxicating personality seems to point to a rich and fulfilling life.

"I believe in carpe diem and making the most of every day," said Bart. "Dad told me, 'If everybody took their problems and put them in a big pile, you would watch what everyone else is putting in and go get yours back out.' It's important to keep everything in perspective. Read your scriptures, and pray over your personal issues and concerns."

Several years ago, Bart was celebrating his fiftieth birthday with close male buddies by drinking beer into the wee hours of the morning. It was after this evening of debauchery that Bart began re-evaluating what was important in his life.

"I knew it was my weekend to be with the love of my life, my son, Cade Black," said Bart. "His mom and I share custody. I was looking awful upon picking him up this day. I knew it was necessary and important to change my behavior."

Bart spent some alone time after this weekend and reflected on advice offered by his dad many years ago.

"When growing up as a kid in Jasper, I experienced a normal, middle-class life," said Bart. "I was blessed with a good family, good community, and great friends in a wonderful neighborhood. The biggest challenges I faced as I got older were making my own choices and dealing with the consequences of them."

Bart admitted to making some unwise decisions during this transition.

"I made some bad choices, but when I became a father eight years ago, I began to realize the consequences of the decisions I made," Bart said. "At the beginning of 2015, I decided it was all on the table. I would leave my comfort zone. And those who know me realize that I don't do change very well. Most of these changes have been positive – many have been challenging – but, hopefully, all will be worth it."

Bart mentioned that one of the hardest things he faces today is trying to live as a Christian.

"Sure, I do Christian things: go to church, volunteer, and help others," Bart said. "But I'm surrounded daily by temptations and bad choices. I will, however, firmly dig my heels in and stand on my faith and allow God to lead me where he wants me to be. God has a plan for me if only I will get out of his way."

What advice might Bart offer to those struggling with big decisions?

"I can only speak to my own experiences," said Bart. "I have no idea what it's like to be in someone else's shoes. But I can share what's in my heart. I can tell my story in hopes that it will resonate with others and maybe help them in some way. But I do realize that not everyone will get it or that it's just not for them. What I can't accept, however, is to sit back and do nothing. That's not who I am or how I'm wired."

So what are some of the changes he's made?

"I quit drinking after my fiftieth birthday," said Bart. "Eight months ago, I quit smoking cigarettes. People will say it's the most difficult thing you will ever do, and I've said that myself. But, in reality, it's not even close. Burying parents, grandparents, family, and friends – those are difficult things. This was simply uncomfortable."

Breaking the habit of smoking is like breaking any bad habit, according to Bart.

"If you can make it one day, you've got it," Bart said. "I knew after that first full day and night I would not go back. Nope, I was done. The hardest day was behind me. Sure, there were more days ahead that presented challenges, but I took them one day at a time. Change is hard, and you might try to resist. Don't be afraid to fail. Don't give up; keep at it; persist. It will get better as you change. And this doesn't apply to just quitting smoking. It applies to any lifestyle changes."

Bart's friendly disposition and personality have allowed him to develop many close and lifelong friends. But he points out that friendship comes with disappointments.

"I value my friendships," said Bart. "A simple thank-you may change a person's day. Everyone should choose their words wisely. Do not let your mouth say what your heart doesn't feel. My advice is also never to hold grudges. Holding onto issues will destroy even the best relationships."

Knowing that families often have issues, it was interesting to hear Bart speak about his relationship with his brother, Gregg, and his sister, Cindy.

"We love one another dearly," said Bart. "We're always there to support one another should the need arise. The same is true for my step-mother, Missy Black. After Mom passed away, Dad found Missy, and they married after dating for five years. Dad loved her, and I do as well, and I told her so on Mother's Day. She's an important person in my life."

Bart is simply fun to be around.

"Nobody wants to hang around negative people," said Bart. "These folks can be down-right harmful to your well-being. Cherish every day, and spend your time with fun and exciting people. I'm aware that my actions could influence someone positively or negatively. One never knows who might be observing your behavior, like your children, so I try to find something good in every situation."

Bart believes in exercise and nutrition for maintaining good health. He works out regularly at the Court House Racquet Club, and he attributes his high energy level to exercise and taking time to unwind after a busy day.

"Everyone should engage in daily exercise," said Bart. "It is good for your health and good for your soul. Your daily routine might involve just a brisk thirty-minute walk in the late afternoon. It's important to do something physical to clear your mind from everyday life stresses."

Bart was active in sports during high school as a kid in Walker County, Alabama. Bart's present day slim and athletic body type makes it easy to envision him participating in football, baseball, and basketball during high school.

His brother, Gregg, said, "Don't let him kid you. Bart was the fastest kid in Walker High School during his time. He was once timed at ten seconds flat in the 100-yard dash. My brother could fly. He can also play a serious game of golf, but he's really a much better fisherman."

In addition to his athleticism, Bart is known in a few close circles to be a bit of a musician. He plays the guitar and has been known to sing on occasion.

"What I do is just pick 'n' grin with friends, but I do more grinning than picking," said Bart. "I do, however, love music. One of the first concerts I attended was the American hard-rock band Kiss in 1980. I remember my dad saying, 'Those guys will never make it.' I suppose even dads can be wrong once in a while."

Like his father, Bart has enjoyed a longtime love affair with the University of North Alabama. Bart loves attending football games on cool fall afternoons. It is always fun to catch up with him during one of these exciting days of fellowship and action between the sidelines. And catch up we did on a crisp fall day in October, when the University of North Alabama Lions were playing the Western Oregon University Wolves.

The UNA fans and friends were tailgating under the alumni tent. I was relaxing in a lawn chair on this gorgeous afternoon when a smiling man and his young son walked up Spirit Hill to join the festivities. Father and son were wearing matching bright purple sweat-shirts emblazoned with the school's letters. The scene could have been straight out of the 'The Andy Griffith Show,' but instead of Opie and Andy heading to the fishing hole, these two were attending a football game.

It was Bart Black and his son, Cade, walking hand-in-hand to join the pre-game activities. Cade Black's eyes were as big as saucers when glancing around at the pageantry. Bart sat down in a chair next to me as his son darted in and out among the many football fans. Within a few seconds, Cade and a few kids began tossing around a UNA football. Bart, drinking nothing but sweet iced tea in a large UNA cup was as content as any person I had seen in recent memory.

Bart leaned over to me and said, "I remember attending my first UNA football game with my dad. Those are special memories. In fact, I recall tossing around a football just like Cade is with his buddies. It doesn't get any better than this."

Within the next few minutes, Cade ran over to his dad after catching a beautiful over-the- shoulder pass from a new friend.

"Thanks for bringing me to the game," Cade said. "Roar Lions! Love you, Dad!"

"I love you, son," said Bart.

Bart pulled down the bill of his UNA visor to hide the tears flowing freely on this special father-and-son afternoon outing.

He said, "Bill, as much as I love football, there are more important things in life. And one more thing: It took me a while, but I'm certain that I have learned the meaning of wisdom. Yes, I know I have. How about another cup of sweet iced tea? I believe I will."

Chapter 13

Mary Graham Garner

$\mathscr{I}$t is nearly impossible to convince the highly active eighty-three-year-old Mary Graham Garner to sit down in her den for a few hours on a Thursday afternoon in late August, but she agrees to do so on one condition: Over the course of the next several hours, our conversation will be interrupted as she goes back and forth to her kitchen to oversee her one-woman operation of preparing food for the dozens of folks who will be fed the next day at the soup kitchen. Mary is featured because of her tireless work and commitment to helping anyone she encounters who is in need of assistance.

Seeing a need and helping to fill it seems to run in Mary's veins. While she puts in an Olympic effort to feed the hungry, her grandfather, John Graham, put in an Olympic-sized effort of his own. Once she settles into a chair and into the conversation, Mary brings out a photo of her granddad; he's pictured with the inaugural United States Olympic team in Athens, Greece, in 1896.

"He was the coach of the first United States Olympic team," said Mary. "After seeing the marathon run in Athens, he returned home to Boston and organized a city marathon. It soon became known as the Boston Marathon."

Mary's granddad was born in Liverpool, England, in 1862, and, during his youth, he was one of the fastest runners in or near that city. An article in the Boston Post dated Feb. 19, 1911, said that American athletics owe much to John Graham.

"He was in charge of the Harvard University track-and-field teams from 1901 through 1904," said Mary. "But his best quality was his modesty. He once saved two men from drowning, and the circumstances of the rescue required immense courage, yet he never once referred to the incident; the knowledge of it came from eyewitnesses. I have tried to live my life in the same manner."

Mary shares her grandfather's energy and drive. Before all of the work she puts into the soup kitchen, Mary spent forty-five years walking, and sometimes running, up and down the halls as a nurse at Eliza Coffee Memorial and Florence hospitals. It might seem hard to believe, but she's even busier in retirement.

It's fitting that Mary would give back to Florence and its residents. It's where she grew up as the only child to John and Ethel Graham.

"Both of my parents were deeply caring individuals," she said. "I vividly remember dad stopping in Atlanta during our vacation to visit a fellow employee from Reynolds Metals, Inc., who was in the burn center of a hospital there. Dad wanted to see if there was anything he could do to help the man or his family. This compassionate act and my parents' giving nature instilled in me a deep concern for others."

After graduating from Coffee High School in 1950, Mary received training at Nashville General Hospital to become a registered nurse.

Mary said, "Nashville General was primarily a training hospital at that time, treating many indigent patients. Most of the doctors were medical students, and some were performing residencies in internal medicine, obstetrics and gynecology, and pediatrics. We were exposed to just about every medical condition you could imagine as part of this on-the-job experience. Nashville General was, at the time, the only hospital in the city with a twenty-four-hour emergency room."

This initial experience was just the start for Mary's medical career. Mary would go on to obtain a Bachelor's of Science degree in Health Care Management from a small college in Windham, Maine.

Mary said, "It was during the mid-1970s, and I had been taking many continuing education courses. St. Joseph's College offered an accelerated course, so I flew to Maine to obtain this additional education and training."

Her first job assignment in Florence was as the assistant director of nursing at ECM Hospital, but, in those days, nurses did whatever was required to assist and treat patients.

"I worked with many outstanding doctors at ECM Hospital," she said. "Dr. John Nofzinger was a brilliant neurosurgeon, but his compassion for patients is what I most admired. We treated many young boys with broken necks from high school football injuries. It was heart-wrenching to see these young boys and their parents being told their sons would never walk again. Dr. Nofzinger insisted on delivering the dreadful news to the patient and families. These memories stick with you forever."

Mary's life took a detour when she was asked by co-worker and friend Bill Watson to move to Guntersville, Alabama, to open and staff a new hospital. Mary, never a person to lack confidence, jumped at the opportunity.

"Bill and I opened Guntersville Hospital in the fall of 1963," Mary said. "Bill was the CEO, and I was the Director of Nursing. We did all of the hiring for the hospital. There were politics involved, but we got the hospital up and running very well. The whole family moved to Guntersville. This included my husband, our four children, my husband's brother, my mom, and our dog."

Mary's best friend and next door neighbor, Betty Burdine, was in the process of moving from Florence just as the Garners were moving to Guntersville. Betty and her husband, Robert "Bob" Burdine, along with their four-year-old son, Greg, moved to Tuscaloosa as Bob had been accepted into The University of Alabama School of Law.

"The first weekend we were in Tuscaloosa, my husband, Bob, insisted we drive to Guntersville to see what Mary was cooking," Betty said. "We did so, and our family stayed the weekend with Mary and her family. I don't recall where we all slept, but the exotic food was delicious. This began a monthly visit to Guntersville. It would be an understatement to say Mary is a fabulous cook."

After a year of satisfying work in Guntersville, Mary and Bill Watson were recruited by a team of doctors to return to Florence to open, staff, and run a new facility. The family decided to move back to Florence, and they have lived in the Shoals since.

Mary's eyes reveal her deep and caring nature as she recalls these days of helping severely injured people. Mary took on the challenge of opening Colonial Manor Hospital in Florence with Bill Watson. Bill was a friend, and he was the administrator for the new facility. This nursing home would later become Florence Hospital, and Mary served as Director of Nursing from day one.

She recalled Dr. Gilbert Melson for his skill and devotion in treating children. He was especially skilled in his unique ability in treating kids with severe arthritis.

"He helped so many kids," Mary said. "We had to use what was known as an Iron Lung as a respirator on many patients. This was an airtight metal tank which enclosed the entire body except the head. If we lost power, we were forced to use the manual controls to keep the patient breathing. We did whatever had to be done."

The skill with which she handled patients, especially those in the last stages of a disease, caused several doctors to request that Mary visit many terminally ill patients in their homes.

"This was the beginning of hospice care in our area," she said. "We did what we could to make the patients comfortable during their terminal illness. Hospice of the Shoals evolved from these early days of treating these patients. I became a board member when Hospice began as a full-fledged operation."

Volunteering for health-related organizations in retirement is just as important as her work in the healthcare field. Mary volunteered for the American Red Cross, Help Center, Hospice, and many other organizations. She has helped the University of North Alabama begin its well-respected nursing program, and she now devotes time to helping the less fortunate at the local soup kitchen.

She said, "The soup kitchen is based out of First Presbyterian Church in downtown Florence, and our church, Trinity Episcopal, is responsible for the kitchen the first Friday and Saturday of the month. Most of us have never gone without a meal and everyone should consider helping these individuals. Look out for others in the community."

In addition to her volunteer work, Mary enjoys a fulfilling personal life. She and her husband have been married for sixty years.

What is the secret to a long and successful marriage? Joe Garner answered immediately.

"It is very easy. I am wrong fifty-percent of the time and Mary is right fifty-percent of the time, so it's simple math. She is right one-hundred percent of the time," he said.

Together, she and Joe have built a family. Mary's eyes beam with pride upon discussing her four children, nine grandchildren, and one great-grandchild. The Garners still maintain a backyard swimming pool, despite Joe's declining eyesight as a result of macular degeneration, for the kids and grandkids to enjoy. Mary does the housework and normally cooks every night.

Betty Burdine spoke about Mary's compassion for others as well as her culinary skills.

"Mary looks out for people, especially elderly folks who don't have family in town," said Betty. "As far as her cooking, my husband would frequently disappear around supper time. I knew he was at Mary's house tasting another one of her fabulous dishes. Mary gives freely of her time and does many things nobody ever hears about. She is a dear friend and an incredible person."

Despite her many accomplishments and devotion to the service of others, Mary remains unassuming and modest. She is not a person to seek attention.

"I don't do anything for recognition," said Mary. "The most satisfying feeling in the world is found in helping other people."

Mary Garner is a remarkable individual. Her devotion to helping others is something to be admired, emulated, and lauded.

What advice would Mary give to others? That's easy: "Get involved in your community. Find organizations that need volunteers. We have many homeless who sleep under our bridges. I personally know some of them. They are good people who experienced some misfortune."

It's clear the topic of homelessness, especially as it affects those locally, is one that inspires emotion in Mary.

"Many people in society look down on the homeless," she said. "I was at a breakfast not too long ago that welcomed these desperate men and women to join us. As Christians, we are not to judge people seeking food, clothing, and shelter. There are many ways we can help the less fortunate improve their way of life. Trinity Episcopal Church has the St. Francis Fund, a project where all funds raised go toward helping local charities."

Mary has spent her lifetime trying to help improve the lives of other people.

"I believe if something is wrong that it's our duty to try and help, so quit complaining and put your energy to work to make the situation better," she said. "Everyone can do something to help, so, instead of talking about these individuals, why not consider listening to them? They have a story like you and me, and you might be pleasantly surprised to hear how fascinating their lives have been."

James "Trip" Triplett

Retired United States Army Major James C. "Jim" Triplett is a fast-talking, straightforward man who served our country in the Vietnam and Korean wars. His stories about his early life and proud military service are spellbinding. Despite working with and for some of the most powerful individuals in the world, the man who goes by Trip makes one thing vividly clear: The people he admires most are those salt-of-the-earth folks like his Aunt Ruby and Uncle John Earp. Trip is included because of his core family values and for being a genuine friend to the ordinary man and woman.

Trip's mom and dad split up soon after he was born on May 20, 1930, in Morgantown, North Carolina.

"I'm told that my dad went to work one day in 1930 and didn't return," Trip said. "This left Mother, my older sister, Billie Sue, my brother, Raymond, and me without any food or money. Mom was a pretty girl but had little education and limited work skills. In spite of Dad leaving, I always loved him. Mom could never understand my affection for Dad and never learned to condone it."

After his father's abrupt departure, Trip and his brother moved in with his Uncle John Earp and Aunt Ruby on a sharecropper farm in Wilkes County, North Carolina. Their sister stayed behind with Mom. Trip considered the Earps as much of his family as his birth mom and dad. Aunt Ruby, Trip's father's sister, offered unconditional love and compassion in her small four-room house on Beaver Creek. The seven Earps and the Triplett brothers lived together in the tiny home without the luxury of indoor plumbing or the many amenities that we're accustomed to today.

"Uncle John had no real education and limited jobs skills," Trip said. "He was a sharecropper and a timber cutter. Despite being poor, he was a deeply caring person who shared everything he owned. The Earp's son, Raymond, became my best friend. We did everything together in the creeks and fields of Wilkes County. Raymond died of an illness at age nine, and his only possession in the world when he died was a 50-cent piece. I was later given this by the family. I have it mounted on my wall as part of a cross-stitched sampler that I stitched. It reads: Raymond Kyle Earl, my first cousin and best friend."

Trip's aunt Ruby would become one of the most influential people in his life. She demanded everyone work hard from daylight until dark. They churned milk to make butter and buttermilk, and the kids carried water to the workers in the corn fields. Other duties included grinding molasses from sugar cane, killing and dressing hogs, razing buildings, and thrashing wheat.

Even the family pet had a job to do, according to Trip.

"He was a pit bull and the best friend a family could have," said Trip. "We called him Old Pal, and he killed rattlesnakes and copperheads, and we never entered the fields without him."

Despite being poor, Trip said his Aunt Ruby always helped others and made sure the family had something to eat, even if it was packed away as a school lunch.

"We left before daylight and crossed a pitch-black muddy hill to wait for the school bus," Trip said. "It seemed like it was always cold and dark on the way to catch the bus. My lunch was a fried potato cake or sliced tomato in a biscuit. I was embarrassed for the kids to see my lunch, but I loved those sandwiches made by Aunt Ruby."

Trip said the family frequently ate possum, rabbit, and squirrel for supper. But when the preacher came, everyone ate fried chicken.

"We would kill a chicken and fry it just before the preacher arrived," Trip said. "Aunt Ruby loved that man and her small country church."

Although Aunt Ruby was a woman of deep and abiding faith, there was little she could do to stop the two boys from getting into things. Trip recalled a visit to the neighbor's house who also happened to be a bootlegger. At just nine years old, Trip and cousin Raymond would enjoy a little homemade moonshine sweetened with sugar and chased with a bite of onion, fresh from the garden, to take away a bit of the burn as the alcohol went down.

"My life was unusual, but many people were good to me," Trip said.

It was Aunt Ruby who taught Trip to be compassionate and humble.

"We had nothing to speak of, but Aunt Ruby would share everything she owned," he said. "There was a homeless man who resembled Santa Claus who came by the house. My aunt said he had lice in his long white beard, so she never let him inside the house. Instead, she gave him food and let him sleep on the front porch. My aunt was one of the most remarkable people I have known."

With the work ethic he learned from living on the Earp farm, Trip was able to work and help pay his tuition at a private Episcopal school by performing odd jobs on campus.

"I worked my way through school to pay tuition," said Trip. "I fired the furnace at five in the morning and cut hay each afternoon after class. My job was also to feed the cows and make sure all the hay was in the barn."

Still, a life in academics wasn't his calling, so after the tenth grade, Trip joined the Army as a private on September 18, 1947. After completing basic training at Fort Jackson, South Carolina, Trip was selected for leadership school, where he graduated second in his class. Trip would later obtain his GED and attend college at Georgia State in Atlanta.

"If young people are unsure about career choices, they should consider the Army," Trip said. "It teaches you everything. Joining the Army forever changed the course of my life."

While training infantry soldiers in Atlanta, Georgia, in 1948, Dan James was in one of Trip's classes. Trip drove Dan and a few buddies to Decatur, Alabama, during a long weekend in order to visit their relatives. Sarah James, Dan's sister, had driven her dad's 1948 Chevrolet from Florence to Decatur to pick up her brother.

"Sarah was the most beautiful girl I had even seen," Trip said. "I was bound and determined to meet this girl."

Several weeks after his first encounter with Sarah, Trip drove, unannounced, to Florence to become better acquainted with her. Trip and Sarah bonded immediately and talked into the wee hours of the morning. When he left after that visit, Trip believed that Sarah was the girl he would marry. His instincts proved correct. The couple wed a year later on June 30, 1950.

"I stayed in the Reeder Hotel during my visit," said Trip. "Clyde Anderson owned the hotel in downtown Florence and, ironically, many years later, my youngest daughter, Susan, would marry Clyde's grandson, Terry Anderson."

Trip's outstanding military career took him many places and taught him many things. He served a three-year assignment as Chief of the Intelligence Data Processing Center at the Pentagon before concluding his career with a one-year tour in Vietnam.

Trip's eldest daughter, Becky Jones, offered a tidbit of information about the family's move to Florence in 1972.

"Before Dad left for Vietnam in 1972, he and mom rented a building on Highway 72 and brought a truckload of furniture from North Carolina to start a furniture business in Florence," Becky said. "While Dad was in Vietnam, Mom got Triplett's Furniture Fashions up and running. Dad retired as a Major after twenty-four years of active duty. On the day he retired, Dad drove to Florence, placed his retirement papers on the file cabinet at the furniture store, changed his clothes, and went to work. Triplett's Furniture Fashions was a wonderful family business until Dad's second retirement twenty years later."

Over the past several years, Trip has enjoyed the many activities offered to senior citizens by the Florence Senior Citizens Center. The Club, as it's known, is on 450 Country Club Drive, which is the site of the former Florence Golf and Country Club.

"I love to shoot pool," Trip said. "Most folks say I talk a good game. Also, the lunches they provide are delicious, and the cost is just one dollar. But you might want to get someone else's opinion about the food because I was in the Army for twenty-four years. I'll eat anything you put in front of me. The Club is such a great benefit for seniors."

Despite a difficult upbringing, Trip's life has been quite a success.

"In order to succeed in life, you have to have a reasonable aptitude, an outstanding attitude, and you have to get a break now and then," Trip said. "I've been blessed to have all three.

"I hope everyone will lead honorable, Christian lives, and honor their father and mother," Trip added. "Find a great partner, and study your Bible, and practice Christian concepts. Learn to be an excellent reader. If you can read well, you can travel the world in your own home. Be on time. There is seldom an excuse for being late. I'm on time for church every Sunday at St. James United Methodist in Florence. Do not be afraid to say, ' I love you'."

Retired Major James Triplett is in the twilight of a life devoted to service and loving others. He has travelled to every state in the country with his wife, two daughters, and his six grandchildren in his motor home.

"Some friends think I'm crazy, but these trips have been the most enjoyable times in my life," he said.

Trip became emotional when reflecting upon his deeply fulfilling life. He also turned philosopher for a moment when discussing what he considers important in life.

"All material possessions are fleeting," said Trip. "It's about family and friends. Tell your loved ones how you feel. Don't become self-centered if you enjoy success. If you see that someone needs help, don't wait for them to ask, just provide it."

Finally, Trip is a man of strong opinions but also an individual with deep compassion for all human beings. Money and fame are meaningless to this man of deep and uncompromising faith.

"It boils down to who you are, not what you do," said Trip. "Are you a person of faith and integrity? Do you care about the less fortunate? These are the basic character traits I admire in people. These values were instilled early in my life by two extraordinary people, my dear Aunt Ruby and Uncle John Earp."

One other person has been the guiding love of Trip's life for the past sixty-four years. That individual is his wife, Sarah James Triplett. Trip became overwhelmed with emotion when reflecting on the life and memories shared with this woman.

"Sarah is the best thing to ever happen to me," Trip said. "She is the best wife and mother a man could ask for. She has remained by my side when I moved the family all over the world. She is an immense blessing in my life, and I love her as much today as the day I married her."

Trip became teary-eyed when reflecting on his family he loves so dearly. Trip's friendships and family are his life, and this provided an opportunity to share the words of a cross-stitched sampler he completed. It reads:

Don't walk in front of me,
For I might not follow.
Don't walk behind me,
For I may not lead.
Just walk beside me,
And be my friend.

Megan Lovelace

egan Lovelace's beaming smile and upbeat demeanor light up the offices inside the Henry Harold Self Field House at the University of North Alabama in Florence, Alabama. She has been the fundraiser for the athletic department for close to three years, and her actions demonstrate an authentic love for the position. This ambitious young lady loves all sports and is humbled by the opportunity to help others pursue their dreams. Her efforts directly impact the scholarship assistance available to many young men and women who, otherwise, might be unable to attend college. Megan is included because of her deep commitment to helping improve the lives of other people.

Megan is the oldest child of two to Jay Todd and Christi Hunt Lovelace. Her brother, Wil, was awarded a football scholarship to the University of North Alabama in 2014.

Without a moment's hesitation, Megan said, "My best friend in the world is my brother, Wil Lovelace. He was the long snapper for the Florence Falcons and now performs this same duty for the UNA Lions. I greatly admire his character, faith, and overall values and principles."

The role her family plays in her life isn't limited to her brother. Megan's mom and dad as well as her grandparents, Bill and Sandra Hunt, have helped get her through some tough times, including an incident during her childhood.

"The local doctors found what they believed to be a shadow of a rare pediatric tumor on an x-ray," Megan said. "I was just two-years old, and my parents and grandparents were emotionally devastated."

Because of how rare the tumor was, the family and local doctors made an appointment for Megan to be seen by specialists at world-renowned Saint Jude Children's Research Hospital in Memphis, Tennessee. Almost unbelievably, the test results came back negative for the life-threatening disease. There was no real explanation for the discrepancy in the test results. Upon reflection, Megan, now in her mid-twenties, can only imagine the pain and emotional trauma this scare must have inflicted on her close-knit family.

"I can imagine, now as an adult, what they must have been feeling," said Megan. "Everything turned out fine, but I still think about how difficult this must have been on my extended family. We're so close."

Megan excelled academically as a student at Bradshaw High School, later Florence High School. She was a member of the National Honor Society, the French honor society and the Math honor society. She won the Kiwanis Club Scholarship for her community service project, which was collecting soda can tabs for the Ronald McDonald House, which houses the patients and families at Saint Jude Children's Research Hospital. Despite these awards, however, her fondest high school memory was of being a flyer on the cheerleading squad. Megan bravely accepted this role as the one tossed high in the air during pauses in the action on the field.

Megan never lacked the courage to perform these high-flying feats, so she executed the stunts, from basket tosses to aerials, throughout her four years at Bradshaw.

"The flyer has to maintain a smile, perform acrobatic moves in the air, and have complete trust in the people below her," said Megan. "The role of the flyer can be risky and requires the individual to be fearless."

After graduating high school, Megan attended Auburn University where she graduated summa cum laude with a degree in communications and a minor in business. She received the Eugene D. Hess Memorial award in 2010, given to the most outstanding communications student. After graduation, she further developed her skills by interning with the Alabama Sports Festival. This festival was organized in 1982 at the request of the United States Olympic Committee to develop Olympic-style competitions and expose athletes and spectators to Olympic sports and their traditions. After this internship in 2010, her aunt mentioned a job opening in her hometown of Florence.

"This was the first job I applied for after my graduation," Megan said. "I was fortunate to be offered the position as community representative for the American Cancer Society. I was thrilled to be working in my hometown around family and friends. I'm proud to say we secured over one million dollars for local cancer patients and life-saving research during my three-year tenure."

Megan loved her experience with the American Cancer Society, but she had always dreamed of being involved in some capacity with sports.

"I heard about an opening with UNA as a fundraiser in the athletic department," she said. "With sports playing such a big role in my family, I applied for and was hired by Athletic Director Mark Linder. This is no 8-to-5 job, but I love being around the positive energy found in our department. The time demands can be overwhelming, but we take a moment every day to count our blessings. Mark creates a positive work environment, and his management style is ideally suited for allowing us to produce results."

Although she has been with UNA for three years, it's clear that Megan has found a career that allows her to follow her passion.

"Many of the student athletes I work with come from broken homes," she said. "Their only hope to attend college is to receive some sort of scholarship assistance. My job is to raise money for these scholarships, as well as capital projects. I feel like I am making a difference in their lives, so it's very humbling."

The modest Lovelace admitted to experiencing her own difficult times, despite the always smiling face, but helping those in need has given her an appreciation for the life she leads.

"Don't be fooled. There are plenty of bad days when I go home and have a good cry," she said. "But I remind myself that many are facing far more difficult struggles than I am. Someone is always fighting a tough battle, and we know little to nothing about their circumstances. I hope my smile helps a few of these disheartened individuals."

People skills are a must in Megan's role at UNA, but she has encountered her share of mean-spirited folks.

"That's an understatement," she said. "My grandmother gave me wonderful advice on those types of people. She told me to kill them with kindness and to be better than them. I try to live my life accordingly."

Work is obviously a high priority in Megan's life, so what advice might she offer to people with demanding careers similar to her own?

"The demands of most full-time careers make finding time for a personal life very challenging," said Megan. "So I think it's important to find a job or career that offers satisfaction and fulfillment. Most of us spend more time at work than anywhere else in our lives. Fortunately, I am deeply blessed to work with remarkable people who are not only my co-workers but friends."

While Megan loves her daily associations with her UNA family, she believes it's important to maintain contact with friends who may have moved away from their hometown.

"It's easy to lose touch with our high school and college friends in this busy world," she said. "But I am determined this will not be the case in my life. There is something special about our closest confidants. I talk to one or two of my best friends, even if for a minute, every single day. You must remain in touch with those people who truly love you."

Laurie Holder, friend with Megan since middle school, said, "Megan is the definition of a great friend. She is kind to everyone and beautiful inside and out. She has the biggest heart and would do anything for anyone she meets. She is a great role model, and I am fortunate to call her my best friend."

While so many in our pressure-filled world often choose to criticize other people, this trait appears to be missing in Megan's vocabulary.

"I know my time is best spent on improving my life instead of criticizing others," she said. "I have more than enough issues of my own to keep me busy."

Rarely has Megan been excluded from groups in high school or college, so what advice would she offer to those who don't so readily adapt in social situations?

"There are outstanding men and women in social clubs and some men and women who are not so wonderful," she said. "This is true in all organizations. These clubs are a small part of life growing up, especially in the South. In no way do they define you as a person. Character is defined by how you behave when no one is looking. How does a person treat the less fortunate? Are they giving back to the community? These are the important concerns by which a person is ultimately judged and remembered."

So many memories in Megan's life are tied to sports, and she loves to reminisce about special moments involving family members and the rough-and-tumble sport of football. Some of these moments are passed down from one generation to another. Megan's grandfather, Bill Hunt, was a star running back for the Coffee High School Yellow Jackets during the school's one-and-only state championship title in 1964. Megan would later cheer in the same arena, Braly Municipal Stadium, and her brother, Wil, now a member of the UNA Lions, played on this field for the Florence Falcons.

With this being said, let's return briefly to a cold, but pleasant, Friday evening in Florence inside Braly Municipal Stadium in 2003 for the final football game between two heated rivals. Because of the recent school consolidation, Coffee High School was playing cross-town rival Bradshaw High School one last time.

On this special night, young men were selected to assist the cheerleaders on the sidelines. The young men, filled with adrenaline, and only thinking about showboating to the crowd, forgot their obligation to catch the cheerleader flyer. Megan, after flying high into the cool night air, came down hard on her lower and middle back. But in a style reminiscent of Kerri Strug, in her famous vault in the 1996 Olympic Games in Atlanta, Megan bounced right up and smiled for the crowd. This best describes Megan Lovelace. She is always, regardless of her personal issues, concerned with inspiring others through her beaming smile and uplifting personality.

Chapter 16

Terry Haddock

$\mathcal{M}$any of you will remember Terry Haddock as the friendly stockbroker for A.G. Edwards in downtown Florence, Alabama. Some of you may recall seeing him playing golf or tennis with friends and family at the local country club. You may have even greeted him at the First United Methodist Church on Sunday morning. What you may not know about Terry is that he was so committed to his role as Sunday school teacher that he stayed home every Saturday night to prepare. Terry is included here because of his impeccable character and his commitment to treating everyone, regardless of his or her status or position in the community, exactly the same.

It was a cold and drizzly night on October 3, 1959, and I was standing next to my father, Dr. S. S. "Tut" Norvell, the team physician, on the Coffee High School sideline in Florence, Alabama. The Decatur Red Raiders, led by head coach, Shorty Ogle, were in town to play the Yellow Jackets.

It was early in the first quarter when number seventeen Charlie Young received the Red Raider punt around his own twenty-yard line. Charlie began running toward the right portion of the field. Suddenly and unexpectedly, he handed the ball to Terry Haddock on a reverse, and the junior speedster sprinted eighty yards down the sideline for a touchdown. The Yellow Jackets went on claim a victory by the score of 41-0. It has been more than five decades since that cold evening, and Terry Haddock remains the best high school football player I have ever seen, and, yet, he was an even better person.

Terry was the middle child of three boys to Gertha and Margaret Haddock, of Florence. By all accounts, he was athletically gifted from an early age. He was involved in a number of sports as a kid and even excelled on the Florence swimming and diving teams. While at CHS, Terry became best known for his skills on the football field. During his career, he was credited with returning an unheard of twenty-one punts for touchdowns. In track and field, Terry won consecutive state titles in the 100-meter and 220-meter events. He was timed at 9.6 seconds in the 100-yard dash. The basketball team relied on his unique skills as point guard for three years running.

In addition to athletics, Terry was extremely popular with fellow students in high school. At a time when arrogance often characterized top athletes, no one seemed to associate that word or behavior with Terry. He treated everyone at Coffee High School with friendly respect. Not surprisingly, Terry was selected as Mr. Coffee High School his senior year in 1961. This was an all-around award and not based on his remarkable athletic accomplishments.

After high school graduation, Terry attended Georgia Tech in Atlanta on a football scholarship and excelled on the field and in the classroom. He received his degree in industrial management. On a spring trip to Auburn in 1965, he reconnected with a former high school friend, Susan Young. The two began dating and were married a year later in 1966 in their hometown of Florence.

What looked to be a promising future in professional athletics with the St. Louis Cardinals was cut short because of a knee injury. Terry had to rely on his intellect, rather than athletic ability, in order to provide for his new wife and what was destined to be a growing family. Terry accepted a management position with Phelps Dodge. His first assignment with the company was in Carbondale, Illinois. In 1974, Terry was transferred to Los Angeles, California, to head up a larger company division.

"Terry and I loved living in Los Angeles," said Susan Haddock. "Everything we experienced during our five years there was utterly fascinating. Jennifer was ten and Brian was six when we left California in 1979."

Times were changing rapidly in the business world when Terry and the family relocated to Columbia, Tennessee, in 1979. The family welcomed third child, Andy, at about the time Terry received a phone call from Charles Moore with A.G. Edwards in Florence.

According to Susan, Terry was ready to move back to the place he called home.

"Terry believed it was time to put down some roots for the kids," Susan recalled. "He prayed about the job offer to be a stockbroker and accepted the job to return to Florence. We came home in 1983 and have never regretted that decision."

Not long after the family relocated to Florence, another change took place. This time around, Terry's faith life, not career, was the focus.

"Our daughter had been visiting the local Methodist church and began taking her dad with her on occasion," Susan said. "One evening, Terry came home with a huge smile and declared, 'I'm joining First United Methodist Church.' I was overjoyed because this was the very church in which I was raised. Terry became a member the next month, and my membership had never been moved."

Terry quickly became an active member of this large downtown church. He served on the administrative board and in many other capacities. He was best known, however, for teaching a Sunday school class to young high school kids. He believed that sharing his life experiences could offer invaluable insights to these young men and women.

"Terry loved teaching Sunday school," Susan said. "He refused to go out on any Saturday night because this time was reserved for preparing the next day's lesson. I also recall that Terry once served as chairman of the administrative board at First United Methodist Church. He really loved the church."

It's clear this commitment paid numerous dividends among his students, according to Susan.

"If my husband chose to do something, he always gave it his all," Susan said. "I am absolutely positive that he touched many lives by teaching these classes. His engaging personality seized the kids' attention, and Terry was well-versed in scripture. Many of his former students have shared messages of faith they learned from Terry."

So who most influenced the core values and principles of Terry Haddock?

"That individual would be the legendary Coffee High School football coach Joe Grant," said Susan. "Terry learned from Coach Grant to treat everyone with dignity and respect. Terry greatly respected this man. Terry remained true to these principles his entire life. He treated all individuals, regardless of status or job title, exactly the same. Bill Curry, a teammate at Georgia Tech, and a person of deep faith, told me that my husband was as fine a person as he had known. In fact, Bill told me he never heard Terry say an unkind word about another person."

Susan Haddock described her husband as being in the middle of everything. He loved visiting with dear friends from high school and college. Telling stories came naturally to the friendly and people-oriented Haddock. Terry loved people, and they loved him in return. He possessed a rare God-given ability to love others and care deeply about them.

"He never met a stranger," said Susan. "People were drawn to his magnetic personality. He was totally unselfish, always looking out for others. I have never met another person like him. He did not have a phony bone in his body."

Too often, it seems, these larger-than-life personalities are taken from us too soon. And that was the case with Terry Haddock. He was diagnosed with cancer at the age of sixty in 2002.

"He didn't change after receiving the news," said Susan. "Sure, he had some down days, but he handled his daily business with the same smile on his face."

His commitment to others, even throughout this ordeal, was evident.

"Terry felt a huge responsibility to his clients for entrusting their hard-earned money for him to oversee," Susan continued. "He went to the office every day to perform his duties. During his illness, we encountered some difficult times in the stock market, and Terry never once worried about our personal losses, but only about his clients' portfolios."

The cancer treatment required frequent visits to Birmingham and the University of Alabama at Birmingham hospital for chemotherapy. Terry never voiced complaints about the sickness and the uncomfortable trips back and forth to battle the disease. Despite losing fifty pounds, Terry remained faithful to his Sunday school class and his church family.

"Terry never once questioned his personal relationship with God," she said. "He was rock-solid in the faith."

Terry was that rare individual who always placed others' concerns above his own. In fact, Susan said, "Even when receiving chemotherapy in Birmingham, he wanted to know how I was doing. Terry was always asking about the kids' issues. He didn't want his illness to negatively affect their lives."

Even later in his life, Terry was remembered for his skill in athletics. He was a member of the Lauderdale County Sports Hall of Fame and was named to the TimesDaily All Sports Millennium Team. For all of these accolades, his demeanor never changed. At times, he seemed embarrassed by the attention.

Let's return briefly to that cold and rainy evening on Friday night inside what is now Braly Municipal Stadium in Florence. Terry, bearing the number sixteen on his jersey, had performed brilliantly in a Coffee High School victory and was being swamped by reporters and deliriously happy football fans. The cheerleaders were running alongside him and praising his outstanding performance.

But in this maze of commotion and noise, he managed to hear a young ten-year-old kid's voice in the crowd: "May I have your chin strap, Mr. Haddock?"

It seemed like the world stood still. Terry's beaming smile appeared, and this modest football star slowly tossed the treasure into my waiting hands. This was Terry Haddock. Despite the praise and attention, he considered a ten-year-old to be every bit as important as the far more recognized people demanding his attention. Terry Edmund Haddock passed away on November 2, 2007, but his memories will remain with us for generations to come.

Cathe Coulter Harrison

Cathe Harrison was a self-described sports fanatic during her days in the mid-1970s at Muscle Shoals High School. She played about every sport that was offered to female athletes at the time. Participating in team sports has the potential to build and develop character, and character is often associated with loyalty, teamwork, work ethic, and perseverance. It is clear from the way Cathe lives her life that she's learned those lessons well. Fairness, honesty, and respect characterize the way Cathe treats others and are the reasons she's included here.

Cathe is the daughter of Joyce Coulter and the late Wayne Coulter. She was raised in Muscle Shoals, Alabama, along with her brother, Jeff Coulter, of Atlanta, and sister, Mona Jackson, of Athens, Alabama.

Cathe seems to have been born with this love of sports.

"If there was a sport to play, I played it," said Cathe. "I loved basketball, volleyball, tennis, track and field, gymnastics, and diving. I competed in several state meets in various sports, including the state track meet my senior year, where I placed third in the 60-yard hurdles. I was voted most athletic my senior year in high school in 1977. While diving was my favorite sport, I loved the team sports because of the camaraderie with the other players. Team sports helped shape me as a person."

After high school, Cathe pursued her college education at the University of North Alabama in Florence, Alabama. While she loved the experience, she took a sabbatical to begin working for First National Bank in Tuscumbia, Alabama.

"Several years after leaving UNA, I married, and the relationship proved to be unhealthy for me," Cathe said. "There were issues, and we divorced within a two-year period. At this time, I began to reflect on my childhood family life. My dad was an alcoholic, and my mom struggled daily to keep the family together, both financially and emotionally. While my parents loved us, we never saw love between them. Hence, there was never a solid foundation created to show us how a loving family was supposed to be. I ached for this foundation in my life."

As fate would have it, Cathe met the man who would provide the missing piece in her life.

"I really believe God answered my prayers in 1985 when he gave me my soul mate, Price Harrison," Cathe said. "We married in 1986, and, at his encouragement, I returned to UNA and completed my degree in accounting in 1989. UNA was the perfect fit for me, and I received a fantastic education and forged deep friendships."

When she and Price decided to have children, Cathe was emphatic about what she wanted to contribute to their family. When reflecting on her childhood and her mother's inflexible work schedule as a nurse, Cathe recalled the frustration she felt when her mom would be unable to take time from work to attend her athletic events. In turn, Cathe wanted the freedom to put her family first, even before her career. The couple decided that the only way these goals could be achieved would be for Cathe to open her own certified public accounting practice.

"When working for other CPA firms to gain experience, I was made to work long hours," Cathe said. "Tax season was especially hard at the time because I had one child, Millie, and was pregnant with Jessie. I missed several milestones in Millie's life as a result and regretted the overtime demands at work. I wanted to be the one to make the decision to work long hours. I didn't want someone telling me I had to do so. I knew then how I wanted to manage my practice. My office motto would become: Your family comes first."

Cathe opened her practice in March of 1993 and has been blessed since. She has remained true to her core values and beliefs. She has never required her employees to work long hours or overtime, even during tax season. After twenty-two years in private practice, her same principles apply. Cathe allows her employees to work around their family activities.

"I believe this makes for a better and more enjoyable work environment," said Cathe. "My office is Christ-centered, and everywhere you look is a reminder of my values."

It is virtually impossible not to be inspired by Cathe Harrison's upbeat and positive energy.

"No matter how gloomy your day may be, you can find joy," she said, even in the face of work-related stress.

Tax season brings its own stressors, especially for accountants tasked with the increased workload. How does Harrison handle this without compromising her company motto?

"I can be demanding, and nerves become frayed during tax season," she admitted. "I simply calm down, take a deep breath, and ask for God's help. By treating everyone in my office with respect, we have higher productivity and more satisfaction at work. We are family."

Who is responsible for helping shape the person she has become?

"That would be my husband, Price Harrison," said Cathe. "I am a hard worker now, but that has not always been the case. It wasn't until I met Price that I learned the importance of being a good citizen. He is an extremely hard worker. Price is a man of high character and honesty. He has instilled in me and our daughters the importance of accountability, responsibility, and initiative."

It is clear the role Price plays in Cathe's life and their thirty-year marriage.

"Price is my Number One encourager in everything I do," Cathe said. "He tells me daily how much he loves me. We have our disagreements like all couples, but he has never belittled me or disrespected me during the hard times of marriage. Price is my inspiration, the love of my life, and the reason for who I am."

Marriage is difficult, to be sure. Even the most stable couples can experience tough times, but Cathe and Price are raising two daughters, and this brings challenges of its own.

She said, "When my girls Millie and Jessie were small, we always recited my favorite Bible verse, which is Psalm 118:24. It reads: This is the day that the Lord hath made. Let us rejoice and be glad in it. We planted the seed for their growing relationship with God. I have been blessed by them every day in my life."

This background has provided a faithful foundation for Millie and Jessie. It has also served the purpose of keeping the stress of parenting at bay.

"We raised our daughters to make wise decisions," Cathe said. "This is not to say they have always done so, but I am blessed than neither has fallen victim to drugs and alcohol. I trust God will protect them, and any worry on my behalf is wasted time."

Both daughters have channeled their energies through various activities, but the one that's most special to the girls is music and performing with the Auburn Singers, the show choir for Auburn University. Their father, Price, who owns Harrison Gunite, a concrete company, offered the explanation.

"I grew up cutting grass from the age of nine," he said. "My girls have done everything except mow grass. I am still mowing grass at fifty-eight. I suppose I should have taken singing lessons. Both can sing and dance like crazy. Heck, Millie was even elected as Miss Auburn by the students to be the official hostess for Auburn University her senior year in 2011-2012."

Like his wife, Price believes that worry is a waste of time and energy. Instead, he chooses to focus on the positives.

"You can't teach an old dog any new tricks," said the plain-spoken Price. "Geez, I never did anything my dad told me to, but, thankfully, my girls seem to listen to me. We have tried to teach them right from wrong, and then it's up to them. By the way, I did one thing my dad told me. He said upon meeting Cathe, 'Son, you ought to marry that girl.' The moral is to listen to your parents because they know best."

Despite being a highly successful business person, Cathe remains an individual of humility and unwavering faith.

"I begin each day by reading my daily devotional," said Cathe. "It's written by the best-selling author Sarah Young, and it is titled 'Jesus Calling.' Her devotional offers me reassurance, comfort, and hope. I also wear a cross somewhere on me every single day. This reminds me of the one who is ultimately in charge of my life."

It has been said that the most difficult job in the world is that of being a mother. Despite the tough decisions required during the child-rearing process, Cathe has navigated this slippery slope while maintaining a loving relationship with her daughters. Jessie Harrison, the youngest of the girls, recently graduated from Auburn University; she has a wonderful relationship with her mom.

"Mom has the biggest heart of anyone I know," said Jessie. "She encourages me to find joy in all that I do. She is my best friend."

Millie, who is in a doctoral program at the University of Texas at Austin, too, has a similarly deep relationship with her mom.

"Mom is an amazing disciple for Christ," she said. "She is a shining example of grace, kindness, compassion, generosity, and selflessness. She dearly loves others."

Cathe's life is one filled with adventure in conjunction with deep and meaningful relationships.

"Other than my family, my friends are what make my life worth living," Cathe said. "I go to Orange Beach, Alabama, every year during Shrimp Fest with a group of high school friends. We call ourselves the YaYas. It is nothing but laughter the whole time, the laughter-till-your-cheeks-hurt kind of laughter. I have another group of high school friends that gets together every Christmas. We laugh, we share, and we smile a lot. We see how our lives have changed over the past year. We have been doing this for thirty years. God has blessed me with all of these girls."

Cathe is further blessed to have close friends dating back to her college days and her sorority. She becomes emotional upon reflecting on these and, especially, her friendship with Paige Cates.

"I was a member of Phi Mu sorority from 1977 until 1979," said Cathe. "I love my sorority sisters, and many are lifelong friends. Paige Cates is one of them. We've been friends since birth, literally speaking, as we were in the nursery together at Eliza Coffee Memorial Hospital. Paige is honest, dependable, and filled with laughter. I truly believe that, if everyone had a dose of Paige, the world would be a better place. She is so dear to me."

Leading the fulfilling and interesting life that Cathe has enjoyed doesn't occur by happenstance. It, like most things worthwhile, comes with commitment to family and friends and a desire to seek joy on a daily basis.

"I wish someone had shaken some sense into me at twenty-five about how to approach life," said Cathe. "It's easy to meander and not pay close attention to the important issues and concerns. That was me in my twenties. But after meeting Price Harrison, I learned the importance of being a good person and appreciating the smallest things in my life. I am grateful for the people in my life that I have and the love and joy they give me. Please find joy in your day."

Cathe ended by offering her feelings on the meaning of a successful life.

"The best feeling in the world is to know you are loved," she said. "First and foremost, everyone is loved by God, regardless of your sins or your circumstances. Claim that! To live a life and know that you are loved means you are accomplished. I am so blessed to be loved by my family and friends. Overall, a meaningful life, I think, is determined by our relationships, not by money or career success. If everything is taken away, but my special relationships remain intact, then my life has been an incredible success."

Chapter 18

Adolph Abroms

Some of you may recall Adolph Abroms from his days as the owner and operator of Abroms Women's Apparel on Court Street in downtown Florence, Alabama. If you are a bit younger, you may have been a student on a Lauderdale County school bus driven by the energetic sixty-five-year-old Adolph during the mid-1990s. If fitness is your priority, you are bound to have spotted the teddy bear look-alike working out each day at the YMCA of the Shoals. If, by chance, you have missed him, you will usually find him eating Saturday lunch with his two sons, Phil and Marty, and his grandchildren at a local restaurant. Adolph is included to share how his Jewish faith shaped him into becoming a man filled with deep compassion toward others.

Adolph's father, Luke Abroms, was a man known for his dynamic personality. He moved his family of four from the Mississippi Delta to Florence, Alabama, in 1932, just as the Great Depression was settling in. Adolph was just a boy of five when his dad took a chance, despite the economy, and opened Abroms Department Store in downtown Florence.

"Mom hired a maid and a cook to take care of me and my sister while they ran the store," said Adolph. "Dad had no formal education to run a business, but he never met a stranger. People flocked into his store because of his remarkable sales ability."

Adolph insisted that his childhood in Florence was not unlike that of most other children; although, unlike many of his peers, the Abroms family is Jewish. As part of that faith, Adolph, at thirteen, celebrated his bar mitzvah after months of study and preparation.

"This is a big deal in our faith," said Adolph. "We are of the Reformed Jewish faith, and all boys and girls celebrate a bar or bat mitzvah at the age of thirteen. Our temple was in Sheffield at the time of my ceremony. I recall going before the congregation and speaking about everything I had learned."

Friends and family are a big part of these coming-of-age ceremonies, according to Adolph.

"Everybody comes to town for this, and we have a nice reception following the ritual," Adolph said. "This certifies that we are now considered a full member of the temple. We bear our own responsibility for all Jewish law, traditions, and ethics from this time forward. It's like becoming an adult in our faith."

For those to whom a bar mitzvah is unfamiliar, the traditions associated with it create wonderful memories for those involved.

"I vividly recall getting a grand total of $15 in gifts after my ceremony in 1940," Adolph said. "My grandson celebrated his bar mitzvah in 2000, and I believe, if memory serves me correctly, that he received around $10,000. I suppose I missed out. Times have changed a bit over the past sixty years."

Adolph attended local schools in the Florence area until his mother felt he should attend Columbia Military Academy, or CMA, his junior year in high school.

"Mom felt that I needed a little more discipline," said Adolph. "I suppose she was right. I was the only kid around with an automobile and was getting out on the town a bit too much. They didn't let us party at CMA. Oh, we did sneak out a few times, but don't tell anyone."

Although he attended four different universities after his stint at CMA, Adolph remained a few credits shy of a degree. Instead of taking on a fifth college, however, Adolph's dad insisted he accompany him to Birmingham. The elder Abroms had closed the Florence store in 1950 and wanted to test the business waters in a larger, more metropolitan city. The family stayed in Birmingham for three years but found the business conditions there to be less than favorable.

"We tried to make a go of it in Birmingham," Adolph said. "Although business wasn't so good, I did meet an interesting young lady named Sybil Cohen. We began dating, and Mom and Dad were tickled to death because Sybil was also Jewish. It was expected that I marry within the Jewish faith, and Sybil's parents felt the same. We hit it off and were married eight months later in 1953."

The family returned to Florence in 1953, and, with the backing of his father, Adolph opened Abroms Women's Apparel in downtown Florence on Court Street. Selling ladies' clothes became Adolph's livelihood for the next thirty years, and, as a result of his devotion, the store flourished.

"The business was good, and Sybil helped me run everything," said Adolph. "Sybil and I took trips to New York City to purchase inventory. I recall staying in a first-class hotel for six nights, attending Broadway shows, dining at Mamma Leone's, and the cost for the entire trip was under $600. Times have changed a bit there, too, I suppose."

The Jewish faith has been the spiritual foundation throughout Adolph's life. The family has always attended the Temple B'nai Israel, initially when it was in Sheffield, but, since 1956, in Florence. Adolph and Sybil are two of the longest standing members in the temple.

"The holiest day of the year is Yom Kippur," said Adolph. "This Day of Atonement falls on the tenth day of the month in the Jewish calendar. We observe this holy day with a twenty-four hour period of fasting and intense prayer. We believe that the fate of each person is sealed for the upcoming year. Don't tell anyone, but I might have my sausage biscuit just before the twenty-four-hour period ends."

In addition to Yom Kippur, there are other traditions and holy days.

"Hanukkah, the Festival of Lights, is an eight-day holiday commemorating the victory of the ancient Israelites over the Syrian Greek Army and the miracle of restoring the menorah to the Holy Temple in Jerusalem," Adolph said. "The miracle is that one flask was found with just enough oil to burn for one day, and yet it lasted for eight full days. We celebrate at home by lighting the menorah, and each night we add one candle until we reach eight. We sing songs, eat latkes, or potato pancakes, and exchange gifts. But it's important to use a little common sense when you are eighty-eight. I don't light all eight candles anymore because, if I did, I'd probably burn the house down."

Within the Abroms family, there are also other traditions. One, in particular, takes place each Friday evening.

"Our life is built around our faith and our family," said Adolph. "We attend services at the temple on Friday evening. Our Sabbath runs from sundown Friday night to sundown Saturday night. Another family tradition is that Sybil and I have the entire family over for dinner on Sunday night. Sybil stills cooks for the group, and it's a special time. There are usually about ten of us."

While there are many differences between Christianity and Judaism, there are also many similarities, especially as pertains to the congregations.

"We are family," said Adolph, referring to the local Jewish community. "We are small in number and care deeply for one another. Our temple welcomes visitors, and our new female rabbi is fantastic. We don't recruit members, but, if someone likes what they see, our rabbi will explain the religion."

Many of the controversies that have plagued Christianity, especially evangelical Christianity, of late, including the issues of homosexuals and women in the pulpit, seem not to have had a similar effect on Judaism, according to Abroms.

"All types of Judaism, except for Orthodox Judaism, ordain women and gay and lesbian people as rabbis," said Adolph. "We, of Reform Judaism, have been ordaining women since 1972. I'm unsure about the timeline on gays and lesbians, but our female rabbi is outstanding."

This inclusive sensibility has come to characterize Adolph Abroms, and many liken his demeanor and physical appearance to that of a teddy bear as a result.

"My husband will give you the shirt off his back," said Sybil.

As if on cue, the quick-witted Adolph began removing his t-shirt, the same t-shirt that he had recently worn during a workout at the YMCA.

"Here, you're welcome to have this one," said Adolph. "It's a bit sweaty, but you and I are about the same size. I've got plenty more work-out shirts."

Without a doubt, Adolph is a character, so how have he and Sybil kept the spark alive throughout their marriage?

"You might not believe it, but I could really dance the jitterbug," he said. "Sybil and I loved dancing at the club. My wife can flat out jitterbug as well."

There has been no stopping Adolph Abroms. At sixty-five, he took on a new role when many are thinking only about retirement.

"I began driving a school bus for the city of Florence and underwent special training to get licensed," Adolph said. "It kept me busy and was kind of fun. I certainly didn't do it for the money. We were paid $20 per day."

So what's the secret not only to a long but a happy and fulfilling life?

"I think the key is to just keep moving," said Adolph. "I help out every morning at Marty's CPA firm in downtown Florence. After lunch, I work out at the YMCA. Sybil is walking every morning at 5:30, and I walk as much as possible. Stay busy and involved in the community."

Adolph's son, Phil, spoke briefly about his dad's engaging personality.

"Dad can be around someone for five minutes, ask them a few questions, and they are friends," Phil said. "Dad introduces me to everyone, and all of them tell me how much they like him. He is a true joy to the world. I'm immensely proud of him."

Adolph is a huge fan of the University of North Alabama and regularly attends football games and basketball games.

"I love going to the games with my sons," Adolph said. "I was there when the UNA Lions won three consecutive NCAA Division II National Championships from 1993-1995. As good as the teams are, the UNA cheerleaders are even better. I love the cheerleaders."

Adolph Abroms is a deeply compassionate man with an intact and vibrant sense of humor. Simply put, Adolph is fun to be around.

At eighty-eight, he's not too shy to demonstrate that he does, in fact, know how to jitterbug. Something keeps him going, and, according to Adolph, the answer is easy.

"It's all about family, faith, and friends," Adolph said. "Remember, all things will change over time. Some friends will unfriend you. Consider it their loss, not yours. Embrace the changes in your faith. They're coming whether you like it or not. With family, new lifestyles may grab your attention. Learn to embrace them with love. If the grandkids get a tattoo, listen to the meaning behind the body art. You might be pleasantly surprised. Oh, and about being included in the weekend lunch plans, that's simple. Just let the kids know in advance that you're picking up the check."

Chapter 19

Jean Martin Bock

There is a flurry of activity going on inside the YMCA of the Shoals in Florence, Alabama. People are asking questions at the front desk; members are coming and going, yet everything seems to be running effortlessly. While Executive Director Jean Bock refuses to take credit, this atmosphere of organized chaos clearly reflects the down-to-earth Midwestern background of the mathematics major from Carlton, Kansas. Jean loves people and especially loves being in a position to help others achieve a more fulfilling and satisfying life. She is included for this reason.

Jean was raised on a wheat farm near Carlton and didn't expect to stay on the farm. However, she never dreamed of living in the South, much less, in Alabama.

"I'm the third child of four to deeply caring parents," said Jean. "Although we didn't have much in material possessions, we never felt deprived. As with all farming families, there were always chores to be done. In addition to all the outside chores that come with living on a farm, one especially fond memory was the Saturday night ritual of getting ready for church the next morning. Dad, sitting in the kitchen on the little footstool he had made in high school, would diligently polish shoes – saddle oxfords, my sister and I had worn all week. We wore our spruced-up shoes every Sunday morning to Carlton Presbyterian Church."

The first eight years of Jean's education were at Carlton Grade School in the small farming community. There were three teachers for the entire eight grades.

"I was either in the same classroom with my brother, Gary, or my sister, Judy, for six of those eight years," Jean said. "With Gary being two years ahead of me in school and Judy one year behind, it seemed like there was always someone close by who could tattle on me to my parents."

At that time, the town's population fluctuated between 200 and 204 people, depending on births and deaths.

"There are a lot fewer now," said Jean. "My guess is that Carlton has at most fifty people today, and this includes my brother, Harold, and my sister-in-law. My elementary class of nine students was the largest in school history. It was Dennis and Danny, the twins; Larry and Lyle; Von and Donnie; and the three girls, Anna, Madelyn, and me. Despite the small size of our school, I believe my education was a good one. After grade school, all of us, except for the twins who went to the city high school in Abilene, attended the larger county high school, Dickinson County Community High School in the small town of Chapman. It didn't matter to us that Chapman was farther away. We didn't want to go to school with city kids. Besides, we lived in the county school district."

Originally named Dickinson County High School, it was established as the nation's first county high school in 1889. During Jean's junior year in 1967, the school with 530 students was renamed Chapman High School.

"It took a while to get to and from high school," said Jean. "We first rode on a feeder bus, driven by a student, to meet the big bus for the ride through Abilene to the other corner of Dickinson County. In total, every school day I spent about two-and-one-half hours on the bus. It wasn't that bad considering we'd visit with each other and help one another on homework assignments."

Jean recalled how awesome it was having the 34th President of the United States, Dwight D. Eisenhower, call Abilene, Kansas, his home. While the five-star general was born in Denison, Texas, he was raised in Abilene and always considered it his home.

"It was exciting during our early years in school," Jean said. "I don't remember how many times he came back to Abilene during his presidency, but I will never forget being in town during spring break my freshman year in college when his burial service was held. Thousands lined the streets along with military police because the service was attended by many dignitaries, including President Nixon, former Presidents Johnson and Truman, and General Omar Bradley, if I recall correctly. I had a good view of the procession from the steps of the Catholic church across the street from the Eisenhower Center. An outdoor public address system allowed everyone to hear the service."

His body had arrived by train on April 2, 1969. The funeral service had been held in the National Cathedral in Washington D.C., but his final resting place is in a small chapel on the grounds of the Eisenhower Presidential Library in Abilene.

"This was a memorable day in my life," Jean said.

Despite being shy throughout her youth, Jean was an outstanding student. Her husband, Bert, spoke because Jean was too modest to discuss any academic awards.

"Jean was valedictorian of her senior class of 130 students in 1968," Bert said.

Jean was focused and always knew that she would attend college. But she was concerned about the expense of a college education. Part of the money dilemma was solved one day when Jean opened a letter while standing at her mailbox.

"It was a congratulatory letter from Kansas State University stating that I had been accepted into the Smurthwaite Leadership and Scholarship House," Jean said. "This was unexpected good news. The scholarship allowed me to pay lower rates, but I was responsible for the day-to-day operation of the house, along with sixty-three other girls. Cooking breakfast became my primary job. I suppose I did okay because nobody complained about their eggs. Our living arrangement was similar to a sorority house but without the frills. We had social functions, much like the standard sorority on campus."

While in college, Jean began dating fellow student, Bert Bock, and they were engaged before their senior year.

"We were married eight days after we graduated," said Jean. "My mother and I made my wedding dress, and Mom made the wedding cake. It was Bert's job to help Mom get the cake to the church basement without a disaster."

Bert said, "It was a multi-layer cake requiring an engineering feat to get it down the stairway to the basement. But we succeeded, and the reception proceeded beautifully without a hitch."

After the wedding, the newlyweds remained at Kansas State for Bert to obtain his Master's degree, and they then moved to Lincoln, Nebraska, where he obtained his PhD in Agronomy and Soils from the University of Nebraska. Jean soon realized that her future home would depend on where her husband accepted employment.

"Bert's offer came as an assistant professor at Auburn University in 1978," said Jean. "And before you ask, yes, we are big Auburn fans. We loved being a part of the Auburn University family. We still have close friends who live in Auburn."

They left Auburn in 1979 when Bert was offered a position at TVA's National Fertilizer Development Center in Muscle Shoals, Alabama. When this federal agency was formed in 1933, one of its core missions was fertilizer research and development. NFDC's fertilizers and technologies have been used throughout the world to help reduce hunger.

"We moved to Florence that year and have been here ever since," said Jean. "After a twenty-five-year career with TVA, Bert retired and has since been in the consulting business. My first job at the Y was working in the business office. When the executive director retired in 2003, I applied for, and was hired in this position. My additional responsibilities required me to embrace new challenges, including building maintenance issues and supervision of staff."

Jean's life reaches beyond the walls of the YMCA, however. Her eyes light up when she talks about her two children, Melissa and Ryan. She feels blessed to be their mom and is over the moon about her only grandchild, Kate, who is three.

"Our daughter was almost three years old when we moved here, and Ryan was born at ECM Hospital," said Jean. "Melissa is a Bradshaw High School graduate, and Ryan graduated from Coffee High School. The schools were bitter rivals at the time. We considered ourselves fortunate to be fans of both schools."

Sometimes, thinking about her children brings out her emotional side.

"I think I have learned more from my children than I have taught them." said Jean. "When Melissa was three years old, she wanted to pack her own suitcase. Ryan, while he may not have liked it, did the same. What I learned was that children, at a very young age, are capable people. There are plenty of opportunities for parents to stand back and watch their children blossom."

While Florence has been home to Jean for thirty-five years, she has been with the YMCA for the last sixteen. And Jean is more enthusiastic about her role at the Y now than she was on her initial day of employment.

"I think with experience comes wisdom," Jean said. "When I applied for the management position, I was in no way naïve about the challenges that come with being in charge. But I knew I wanted to help make a difference in this world. Without taking the risk that comes with added responsibility, I knew I would never be truly happy. Despite being told I was a long-shot to be selected, I was offered the job. The last twelve years of my life have been deeply fulfilling and satisfying. I have a front row seat to see the difference the Y makes in the lives of so many people."

Jean is quick to point out that many employees play a role in bringing about positive change in the Y's members.

"We have just six full-time employees," said Jean. "However, our one hundred twenty part-time employees are crucial to the Y in so many areas. Each person brings unique skills and uses them to assist our 7,500 members. Our staff is incredible."

Jean would be remiss not to mention the child-care programs offered by the Y.

"Our child-care programs fill a need in the community," Jean said. "We have over 160 kids in our after-school child-care program. We involve them in exercises and various other activities and make sure they begin homework assignments before they are picked up by parents later in the day. We also have children here during summer day camp. These programs are a great help to working parents."

Having responsibility over so many people and so many activities would seem to be a highly stressful occupation, but Jean takes it all in stride.

"I trust that our employees are trained to fulfill their duties," said Jean. "Our men and women do a remarkable job. It's a comfortable feeling knowing how skilled our employees are in so many specific areas."

With so many members and so many employees, Jean said she's adapted her management style.

"I believe in hiring good people and letting them do the job they are hired to do," she said. "I do not micromanage employees. I do not hire 'yes' people. The communication lines are open. We have issues, but they are few and far between."

Of course, the facility and equipment aren't just for members. Jean said she uses them, too.

"Yes I do," said Jean. "I do thirty to forty-five minutes of aerobic exercise five times a week. I also take a yoga class."

The exercise helps keep her fit, Jean said, but she's not competing with the younger folks who work and exercise there.

"Well, no, but I did run my first ever 5K in 2013 at the age of sixty-three," said Jean. "I actually ran another one that year, and my time was pretty good I suppose. I finished first in my age group, but there weren't that many participants in the over-sixty category."

Jean currently serves on the Small-and Mid-sized YMCA CEO Cabinet. The eighteen members are charged with making recommendations to the YMCA of the USA on issues that are deemed important to Ys of this size.

"It's an honor to serve," said Jean. "It's helpful because we network and brainstorm many issues that are shared by all of us throughout the country. It is wonderful to have people to call on when issues arise. We are able to share experiences with one another and can offer invaluable advice."

The YMCA of the Shoals is open for business seven days a week, and rarely do things slow down because of its volume of members. Even on this Friday evening in December, the Y is a bustling hub of activity. Children are being picked up by parents, and the members are getting in that last workout to complete a busy week. Amid all of this, a fit lady, bearing little resemblance to a senior citizen, sprints into the lobby after a rigorous workout. Jean Bock, standing in the background, allows a smile while observing a smooth-running operation. What might she be contemplating as she watches another successful week draw to a close?

"What I notice is that we are a diverse group who feel comfortable enjoying the benefits provided by the Y," said Jean. "Everyone is welcome, and some who are unable to afford the full price for membership and programs receive assistance from public donations. The Y's focus areas are youth development, healthy living, and social responsibility. Everything the Y does relates to at least one of these three categories.

"It warms my heart to see members working to lead healthy lifestyles not only by exercising but also through social engagement. Fellowship, making new friends, and reconnecting with old friends are especially important for our senior members. Watching this gives me satisfaction and brings deep contentment. I am truly honored and humbled to be playing a role in making a difference."

Ronnie Pannell

$\mathcal{R}$onnie Pannell grew up in a house on the steep hill in Florence, Alabama, just above the tennis courts on Royal Avenue and a stone's throw from Braly Municipal Stadium. He enjoys a deep love for the city that has been his home since birth. Ronnie graduated from Powell Elementary School, Appleby Junior High, Coffee High School, and the University of North Alabama. He has done many things in the community, but he is probably best known for his long-time association as teacher, coach, and broadcaster for the Mars Hill Panthers. He is featured among the group because of his deep Christian faith and his motivational spirit that has touched so many people in a positive way.

Ronnie's humorous side surfaces easily and often throughout a conversation. He and I met for a late lunch on a Wednesday afternoon, and, before we'd placed our order, it was clear his company would be enjoyable.

"You know, three of the schools I attended are now closed," he quipped. "I suppose I messed them up so bad they had to shut them down."

Ronnie is the oldest of three boys to Dene and Nell Pannell, of Florence. Gary and Barry, his twin brothers, were born when Ronnie was nine.

Ronnie possesses a natural gift for storytelling which should come as no surprise to anyone who knew his father and his uncle, Gene Pannell.

"Dad and Uncle Gene were twins and well-known for being fascinating storytellers," said Ronnie. "There was never a dull moment when those two were around. Both are deceased, but my mom, Nell Pannell, is eighty-five and doing well. Mom has an astonishing work ethic and handled taxes for clients from 1948 until she retired in 2011 at the age of eighty-one. She is an incredible person."

It would seem that Ronnie inherited his mother's work ethic because he has been working in some capacity since the age of seventeen.

"Coach Press Robbins hired me to help out in Little League baseball," said Ronnie. "This was a big deal in those days. He used me to prepare the baseball fields, cut grass, and line the fields with chalk. I also served as a coach and umpire during my tenure. Those were good times."

Ronnie received his degree in education from the University of North Alabama in 1978 but was unable to land a teaching job. He was hired by the city of Florence in the gas department, and he worked there from 1978 until 1987.

"My wife, Kathy, and I were raising three sons, Jon, Will, and Jeffrey, and my future appeared clear," he said. "But one day, at Jackson Heights Church of Christ in 1987, an elder named George Echols, felt that I might be suited for church work. The church offered me a position as youth minister, I accepted, and the course of my life was forever changed."

How, then, did broadcasting become part of Ronnie's life?

"Greg Thornton, my old buddy, asked me to be a spotter when he was announcing UNA games in 1983," said Ronnie. "I was sold when Greg told me that I got in the game for free and was entitled to all the free food I could eat. The next year, I began calling the games with Greg. We did this for five years until the radio contract expired."

Not long after, Ronnie was able to put his education degree to use when Mars Hill Bible School called in 1991 in need of a history teacher. He accepted the position but continued in a part-time ministry role at Jackson Heights until 2001. In his first season at MHBS, Ronnie coached 36 games and broadcasted 64 games, for a total of 100 sporting events. This was in addition to being a full-time history teacher.

"My energy level was good at that time," Ronnie said. "Those were long but deeply fulfilling days. I was broadcasting basketball games, and my coaching responsibility was the girls' softball team. Many of the girls were also students in my history class, and some knew me from my youth minister role at church. I have baptized several players and students, conducted funerals for some of their family members, and performed weddings for many of my young friends. It's an honor and privilege."

All of this service to others paid off in 2012 when the humble Pannell was inducted into the Lauderdale County Sports Hall of Fame. But Pannell had his share of accomplishments on the playing field, too.

"I suppose they realized that I scored the first ever defensive touchdown in the Coffee/ Bradshaw series," Ronnie said. "My memory is vague, but I grabbed an interception and ran thirty-six yards to pay dirt to help Coffee prevail by a 36-15 score. Steve Pierce, a Bradshaw linebacker, says that, had he been in the game, I would never have scored.

"On a serious note, I was humbled to be inducted for my broadcasting abilities. I talk a better game than I played."

A friend and Mars Hill fan, Todd Thompson, recalled Ronnie's radio broadcasts, calling the action for his beloved Panthers.

"Listening to Ronnie Pannell on the radio is wonderful," Thompson said. "Hearing him talk on adversity and spiritual maturity is even better."

Adversity and spiritual maturity are two subjects about which Pannell knows a fair share.

In 2005, he and his family experienced a loss that many describe as among the worst pains associated with the human condition. While deeply emotional, Ronnie didn't shy away from discussing the loss of his son, Will Pannell, in a tragic drowning accident on June 13, 2005. Will lost his life as a result of the dangerous currents below the low-head dam on Cypress Creek.

"The pain of losing a child is unfathomable," said Ronnie. "It's not the natural order of things. My brother, Barry, died when he was nine from cancer. Mom and Dad helped us a lot. My dad always said, 'When you lose a parent, you lose the past; when you lose a child, you lose the future.' My wife, Kathy, and I have found this to be true. We see Will's friends getting married and having children. We'll be unable to share these joyful occasions with him. We question why, but this answer will come later, and God knows how we feel. He lost his son as well."

As a result of the accident that took Will's life, Ronnie and Kathy Pannell felt a responsibility to bring attention to the dangers associated with the low-head dam on Cypress Creek. Ronnie was aware that his efforts wouldn't lessen the pain of his son's death, but he believed they might prevent future tragedies from occurring at this location.

"Four other people have drowned as a result of this unsafe structure," said Ronnie. "We worked tirelessly for years to convince the city of this danger. The city of Florence, finally, nine years after the tragedy with our son, completed modifications to make the creek safer. We believe our efforts will save future lives."

Throughout the tragedy, Ronnie has maintained a presence at Mars Hill Bible School, and it, in turn, has afforded him the opportunity to touch many lives in a positive manner, and not just through his broadcasts.

"I love teenagers, I love sports, and I love teaching Christianity," Ronnie said "I enjoy seeing our students do well, but, most importantly, I love seeing them grow in the Christian faith. Our motto at Mars Hill is based on Luke 2:52, which talks about Jesus growing in stature and in wisdom with God and man. I'm seeing the next generation return to MHBS, and it's enriching to witness them leading such Christian lives. If my efforts have had a tiny influence in their lives, then I am blessed and humbled."

"My family and my faith are the most important things in my life," said Ronnie. "I was blessed to watch my sons compete in sports, and my calling the action added to the experience. As far as Kathy is concerned, she has always been the wind beneath my wings and my greatest supporter."

Perhaps there is one event that stands out above the others in the remarkable broadcasting career of Ronnie Pannell. It was the 11th of January in 2010, and it was Ronnie's 1,000th broadcast as the voice of the Panthers. He was comfortably settled in his perch above the Panther Den preparing for the first game when he noticed a few students entering the arena wearing t-shirts that read "WILLPOWER."

"I wondered where they got the t-shirts, and my first thought was that I wanted one," said Ronnie. "But my job was to focus on the task at hand."

Within the next few minutes, the Mars Hill Lady Panthers bolted onto the floor, and each player was wearing a red t-shirt over her uniform with the number 31 and the phrase "WILLPOWER" emblazoned on it.

"The team and the school were honoring my family, and, most importantly, my son, Will," said Ronnie. "I was overwhelmed by the genuine love displayed by the Mars Hill family, but I had a game to call. Mike Mitchell, on behalf of the school, presented me with an award for my 1,000 broadcasts after the girls' game. I then returned to the booth and prepared to call the boys' game with Jim Lancaster by my side as always."

Within minutes, the MHBS boys' team erupted onto the floor wearing the same number 31 on a blue t-shirt with the phrase "WILLPOWER."

"Will's high school number at MHBS was 31, and my high school football jersey number was 31," Ronnie said. "Jay Mitchell, our baseball coach, had initiated this idea of the shirts and the phrase, and our family has been humbled by the honor."

The man who was so touched that evening five years ago has influenced many lives by his teaching, coaching, broadcasting, and by sharing his spiritual strength with others. But, on this special evening, his many friends returned the favor.

Before concluding our visit, Ronnie insisted on sharing a few parting words.

"I realized on the evening of the 1000th broadcast that every life will be affected by pain and grief," he said. "So we must put aside any petty stuff and enjoy and love one another during the good times in life. If you can't be happy during these times, then when can you be happy? When grief arrives, and it always does, we must remember one important thing: There is no time limit on this process that claims a piece of our hearts forever. Lastly, I tell my students something that has become known as Coach Pannell's quote, which is: It's never right to do the wrong thing and never wrong to do the right thing."

Chapter 21

Amy Chandler

$\mathcal{A}$my Chandler still beams the same smile that served her so well during her cheer-leading and performing days while a student at Coffee High School in Florence, Alabama. She is the picture of courage and determination. Despite the smile and brave face, Amy is keenly aware that life can change in the blink of an eye. She sustained a life-threatening brain injury in 2003 while living in Vail, Colorado, and has been working diligently to piece her life back together since that tragic day. Amy is included here because of her positive attitude and deeply caring spirit that never fails to provide inspiration to others.

Amy grew up as the youngest of three children to the late Jett Chandler and Jeanette Chandler. She described her parents as hard-working and down-to-earth people.

"My mom's deep compassion for others and my Dad's easygoing manner helped shape the person I have become," Amy said. "They have always been there for support and encouragement."

As she reflected on her four years at Coffee High School, Amy beamed with enthusiasm over her time spent as a cheerleader.

"I loved being a cheerleader at Coffee," Amy said. "I was also involved in show choir and the theater. David Hope, the speech teacher at Coffee, was a huge influence in my life. Because of his encouragement and assistance, the University of Alabama offered me a scholarship in speech and debate."

Despite the scholarship, Amy didn't feel settled and in her element while in Tuscaloosa at Alabama. It wasn't long before she was attending the University of Montevallo in Montevallo, Alabama.

"I found my niche and loved everything about this liberal arts school," she said. "I became deeply involved in theater and arts, and I choreographed my first show. I completed my degree in mass communications and theater in 1995."

Amy moved to Vail Valley, Colorado, after her graduation from Montevallo.

"I was uncertain about what I wanted to do with my life," she said. "But I ran into Martha Osborne, a dear high school friend, and she needed a roommate in Colorado. I jumped at the chance to accompany her. She stayed for a single ski season, and I stayed for ten years."

Amy said she loved the people and the energetic lifestyle found in Vail. She especially enjoyed rafting the rivers, playing golf, and camping in the majestic outdoors. Her career was in retail, primarily a high-end antique store, as well as the fast-paced world of restaurant management. Life seemed to be settling into a routine, but it all changed in a moment on November 3, 2003, when she fell down two flights of concrete stairs.

"I didn't realize the seriousness of my injury until several days after the fall," Amy said. "A doctor from Denver was called in to perform emergency surgery for major skull fractures that were life-threatening. I was experiencing swelling on the brain and was bleeding extensively. The diagnosis was a severe traumatic brain injury. My friends later told me this surgeon saved my life."

Recovery was slow, but, true to her spirit, Amy recovered, and, to a degree, she recovers still. She's unable to work, however, as a result of the problems associated with traumatic brain injury.

"I remember the unbearable isolation and frustration of being unable to perform basic tasks," she said. "After six months in my Colorado apartment, I returned home to Florence to be with Mom and Dad."

Amy experienced a difficult time reuniting with old friends in Florence while trying to piece her life back together.

"Folks at home are largely unaware of the struggles I have endured to be where I am," Amy said. "Everyone was expecting the old Amy Chandler, but this was impossible because of the nature of my injury. Most people believe that, because I look normal, everything is fine. This is a misconception about brain injuries. They are real, and they are debilitating."

Knowing she was never going to be the Amy Chandler people remembered left her feeling hollow and isolated, she said.

"I found myself having pity parties, but I was the only one in attendance," Amy said. "It was a confusing time, but I realized that all the pity and moaning wasn't going to solve anything. I pulled myself up by the bootstraps and began living the best possible life under the circumstances."

During this time, Amy was dealing with a personal issue that had the potential to cause a great deal of stress. She had asked her landlord to donate a few of her belongings to a local thrift store. As a result of a misunderstanding, everything she owned was given away. This included a gift, an early 1800s European antique dresser, which was a bonus for her hard work at the antique store in Colorado.

"The only personal items that I had left after the misunderstanding fit inside one medium-sized suitcase," Amy said. "I was on the verge of a meltdown when my deeply spiritual father came for a visit. He said, 'Amy, I believe in you.' His encouragement was all I needed to move forward in my life. Sometimes, we just need encouragement from a person we admire. Mine came from my incredible dad. I miss him every day."

Despite the ongoing health crisis as well as the mix-up with the thrift store, Amy still found a silver lining.

"I later found the drum stick in my suitcase which was given to me by the drummer of my favorite musical group, Train," Amy said. "After playing 'Drops of Jupiter' in a 2004 Montgomery, Alabama, concert, the drummer, Scott Underwood, flipped his drum stick to me. At least I've got that going for me. It's in my lock box at the bank."

Like the trademark smile, Amy's sense of humor is still intact. She is a self-described free spirit who once auditioned to be on 'Survivor.'

"It was in 2002, before my accident, that I produced a video," she said. "I was swimming fully clothed in ten-degree weather in the Eagle River in Vail. It's what folks around here would call a creek, and ice was covering both sides. There was a tiny slice of water in the middle, and I was swimming like crazy. The 'Survivor' producers liked my promo and seeing me standing in frozen shoes after the swim, but I just missed the final cut. I would have loved competing on the show."

It has been more than a decade since the tragic accident that altered Amy Chandler's life, yet she seems intent on living life to the fullest.

"When I am really down, I look for anything positive in my life," Amy said. "At times, this can be difficult, but, if you keep searching, I believe everyone can find something to be thankful for."

Amy finds enormous joy in singing with the choir at Northwood United Methodist Church. She has been a member there throughout her life. In fact, she was recently asked by Linda Young, the choir director, to perform a solo.

"I'm a terrible singer, but, for some reason, I agreed to this," she said. "My nerves were giving me fits. But when the time to sing arrived, I felt a calming presence. I heard God speak to me saying, 'I am with you now, and I was with you then'."

Among the lingering side effects of a traumatic brain injury victim are depression, anxiety, mood swings, and a lack of communication skills. Coping with these symptoms can be a challenge, Amy said.

"I know that my life will never be the same as before the injury," she said. "My brain and my heart will often feel a total disconnect. This is not unusual for patients with severe brain injury, but I finally know that, after twelve years, my heart is the same."

Amy's faith has kept her going she said, and it's often a powerful inspiration to others facing hardship in their lives. The injury may have slowed her words ever so slightly, but her intoxicating spirit has not been compromised. Her road to recovery has been a lonely and gradual process, but she now feels totally comfortable being the new and, quite possibly, improved Amy Chandler.

"I believe this conclusion has come with age," she said. "Most of us are conditioned to worry about how others perceive us as human beings. It has taken me a lifetime to come to grips with this myself. But finally, I have completely given up being concerned about what others think of me. It doesn't matter if they believe me to be on drugs or fabricating the extent of my injury. I must admit that not as many people like me, but the ones who do are authentic. The people who love me for who I am now are important."

Like every one of us, Amy has been searching to discover who she is by trial and error. Perhaps she has discovered that she was always that person, singing and dancing to the lyrics of "Drops of Jupiter" by her favorite band, Train. Here are a few words from the chorus:

But tell me, did the wind sweep you off your feet?
Did you finally get the chance
To dance along the light of day
And head back to the Milky Way?
And tell me, did Venus blow your mind
Was it everything you wanted to find?

"I believe we should all dance along the light of day and into the evening," Amy said. "While my abilities are not what they used to be, I still love dancing and performing. Dance to your own beat, and do what makes you happy in life. And remember the words of Mother Teresa who said, 'In the final analysis, it is between you and God; it was never between you and them anyway'."

Chapter 22

Tony Kalliath

*H*ow does a bright young man from a country with a population of over 1.2 billion people come to reside and raise his family in the small town of Florence, Alabama? You will soon discover how Tony Kalliath came to practice medicine and help so many in our community who are facing cancer and other blood-related disorders. For this very reason, Tony is included in this endeavor.

Dr. Anthony "Tony" Kalliath was born and grew up in the State of Kerala in Southern India. This part of India is the "Spice Coast" that Christopher Columbus was looking for when he set sail and discovered America. Tony's father, Jacob Kalliath, was the president of a local bank, and his mother, Alice, although well-educated, stayed at home to raise the family. His family's Christian roots trace back two thousand years to St. Thomas the Apostle, who brought Christianity to India, and the church he founded is today known as Syro-Malabar Church.

"Two thousand years ago, my great-great-ancestor Kalliath was a temple priest and one among the first five families to embrace Christianity when St. Thomas first preached the Gospel in India, which, according to tradition, is believed to be in 52 AD," Tony said. "Our church is now in full communion with the Roman Catholic Church. Eighty percent of Indians are Hindus, and Christians are a small minority – 2.3 percent – but we have been Christians from the time of Christ."

After attending private schools run by European missionaries, Tony was accepted to St. John's National Academy of Health Science in Bangalore, India. St. John's is one of the top-ranked medical schools in India.

"I always wanted to be a doctor, and my Dad nudged me along in this direction because of my strong aptitude in science," Tony said.

Why, then, the move from the bustling metropolis of Bangalore to the tiny-by-comparison town of Florence?

"My grandmother and my wife's grandmother were good high school friends," said Tony. "My wife, Molly, grew up in New York City but went to India for her college education. The two grandmothers felt we might be a good match for each other. They introduced us, and we hit it off instantly. We were married six months later and moved to New York City for my residency and fellowship training."

Tony put in grueling hours to complete his training to become an internal medicine doctor and then specialize in hematology and oncology. His additional training in the United States took six years. He then accepted a position with the Veterans Administration Hospital in Brooklyn, New York, and settled there with Molly and their two children.

"We had no plans to move until I happened to see a note on the hospital bulletin board saying doctors were needed in Florida, Arkansas, and Alabama," said Tony.

Tony said that his position at the hospital in Brooklyn had become mundane, so he explored this opportunity.

"I called the number, and the lady at Humana I spoke with insisted they needed an oncologist in Florence, Alabama," Tony said. "I didn't think much about it, but the lady kept calling my wife. We decided to fly down for a visit in 1988. The Humana staff treated us wonderfully, but, most importantly, I noticed the traffic was far more tolerable than in

Brooklyn. We were sold on the area. I accepted the job, and our family of four moved to Florence. Our third child, Matthew, was born at ECM Hospital in Florence. Oh and, yes, the traffic is much better here."

Tony made it clear that he enjoys all aspects of living in Alabama.

"We live on the lake and enjoy those benefits," he said. "I would never trade places with some doctors I know who are still practicing in New York City. I can see patients in all three Shoals area hospitals and still be in my office by 9:30 in the morning. This is impossible in New York City."

Dr. Kalliath opened a private practice in 1989 in Florence, which became the Blood and Cancer Center. It is clear that he is proud of his highly skilled staff of fourteen employees.

"I feel a bit lucky in my hiring process," Tony said. "Some of my staff have been with me for twenty-five years. My people are outstanding in their specific areas of expertise. I have never fired an employee. We work together for the benefit of our patients. I guess I'm biased, but I believe we have the best team in the area for the treatment of cancer and blood disorders."

This highly specialized treatment clinic draws patients from Northwest Alabama, Northeast Mississippi, and Southwest Tennessee. The motto of the facility is: You are not alone. The goal is to treat each patient as an individual, each of whom has a unique set of needs and circumstances.

"We are involved not only with the patient's physical well-being but also their psychological and social needs," said Tony. "Our staff is devoted to helping the family through the diagnosis and treatment process. Our team approach is crucial in helping the patient and the family on the road to healing."

Still, the diagnosis and treatment process are emotionally fraught. Helping patients through this part is just as important as helping them heal.

"In the majority of cases, there is something we can do to help," he said. "Fifteen years ago, on the cover of 'Time' magazine was a pill with the caption 'Cure for Cancer.' This pill was Gleevec, which revolutionized the treatment of cancer. Gleevec is changing the treatment of cancer just as penicillin changed the treatment of infectious diseases.

"Unlike chemotherapy that destroys both good and bad cells, Gleevec works like a magic bullet, targeting the signal that causes chronic myeloid leukemia, or CML, cells to grow. Because of this drug, CML, which causes death in two to three years, can now be kept under control in the majority of patients. The Human Genome Project, funded by the federal government, was the impetus that led to the discovery of drugs like Gleevec, Rituxan, and

Herceptin. There is a plethora of new targeted agents for a variety of cancers and chronic diseases like rheumatoid arthritis and other autoimmune disorders."

Dr. Kalliath went on to describe the four categories of cancer patients he sees in his office.

"The first category involves cancers that can be treated and cured," said Dr. Kalliath. "The second includes cancers that can be treated, but never cured, yet these patients often do well and live normal lifespans. The third category is cancers that are treatable, but the patient will die of the disease. We can often prolong life on these patients for several years. The last category, which includes cancers such as pancreatic cancer, is sadly a group of cancers for which as yet we have no effective treatment. We can offer pain relief and maybe extend life for a few months."

The emotional nature of the disease can sometimes be difficult for Tony, as it is for the patients he treats.

"It is difficult, especially when the patient is young," he said. "Many years ago, I had a twenty-four-year old man diagnosed with chronic myeloid leukemia. This was before the revolutionary drug Gleevec, now available to prolong life. This man, a husband with a young wife and two children, elected to have a bone marrow transplant, which was the only known curative treatment for CML at that time. He died shortly after the transplant, when he was twenty-five. If he was in my office today, we could have saved his life. I still often vividly see him and remember him and his family when I diagnose new cases of chronic myeloid leukemia."

Is it possible to detect this disease?

"Everyone must listen to their body," said Tony. "You know what feels right, and, if you are having unusual symptoms, get to you primary doctor. Blood work will reveal many potential disorders. It is important to get regular tests and screenings. Everyone should know that an early diagnosis increases treatment options and survival rates."

By glancing around Tony's office, I noticed some older photos of him playing basketball and soccer. The humble doctor was reluctant to discuss his athletic days, but a photo of his jump shot revealed a striking resemblance to a well-known player from French Lick, Indiana, one Larry Bird.

"I guess I was a pretty good basketball player in high school and college," he said. "I was also the captain of the basketball team of my medical school. My high school and college coaches insisted that I play goalkeeper in soccer because of my height and agility. I suppose I did a pretty good job defending our goal."

The Kalliath family has been active members of St. Joseph's Catholic Church since moving to Florence. It is clear how important family is by the expression in Tony's eyes when he speaks about them. He displays immense pride yet remains so humble when discussing the remarkable accomplishments of his three children.

"Our oldest son, Jacob, is a medical doctor and is doing his residency in Chicago," said Tony. "Our second child, Lia, just completed dental school and is working in Chicago. Matthew recently graduated from medical school and is beginning his residency in general surgery in Pennsylvania. Our children are a blessing in our lives."

At a time when everyone, especially members of the medical community, faces enormous daily pressures, Tony maintains a friendly disposition and a genuine concern for other people. He and his wife have embraced the Shoals as their home, and the area has clearly returned the favor. None of his children presently live in Florence, and he is hoping at least one of them will come back to practice in the Shoals after their training.

Tony offered a few words about the area he and Molly will always call home.

He said, "Molly probably misses New York City a bit, but she has come to love the area. Downtown Florence just gets better and better with the fabulous restaurants and musical venues. I suggest to all of my friends in the United States and abroad to check out Muscle Shoals Sound and this unique area referred to as the Shoals. As far as seeing the kids, Molly and I love to travel, so we are always ready to go."

Tony concluded with words by the individual who led India to independence and inspired movements for civil rights and freedom across the world. Mahatma Gandhi said:

Keep your thoughts positive because
Your thoughts become your words.
Keep your words positive because
Your words become your behavior.
Keep your behavior positive because
Your behavior becomes your habits.
Keep your habits positive because
Your habits become your values.
Keep your values positive because
Your values become your destiny.

Michelle Rupe Eubanks

espite her many accomplishments, Michelle Rupe Eubanks radiates a profound humility. You simply feel good being around her. She is kind, compassionate, brave, and possessed of deep moral character. A brief visit with Michelle will literally brighten your day. What accounts for this radiant and authentic charisma? It's because Michelle, with her journalist background, is interested in anything and everything, except, perhaps, herself. We could all learn from her and her attitude that seems to say that life is too short to take ourselves too seriously. She is featured here for this reason.

While enjoying a delicious lunch of Brussels sprouts and a black-and-blue burger in a cozy downtown Florence, Alabama, restaurant, Michelle's outlook on life surfaces immediately.

"I'm in a perpetual state of tiredness, so I've learned to just let things go. What's the point of worry and stress, anyway," Michelle said. "On a completely different note, I'll bet you already knew that my husband, Jeff, is a professional chef, but the only two things I can make are pancakes and mac 'n' cheese from a blue box, which my children prefer to his. Go figure."

Intellectually curious from an early age, Michelle developed a fascination with learning about anything and everything, except, perhaps, meal preparation.

"Most kids, when they are little, ask their parents for money, but I asked for books," Michelle said. "I loved reading fiction and non-fiction. I would even open the encyclopedia to a specific letter and devour everything in that section. I've enjoyed a lifelong fascination with learning."

Michelle experienced an unusual childhood as her parents divorced when she was a baby. Her dad, Bill Rupe, remained in Indiana, while her mom, Mary Rupe, relocated Michelle and her sister, Amy, to Florence. Michelle's dad was absent during much of her childhood, but something changed when she became a teenager.

"I suppose the divorce didn't work out because mom and dad remarried when I was thirteen," said Michelle. "They have been married since. Both have been loving and supportive. Although I love to read, I have been and remain a social individual. I wanted to experience everything I was reading about, so I became involved in many activities beginning in high school."

Michelle attended Hibbett School, which then was for kindergarten through eighth grade, Coffee High School, and the University of North Alabama. She served in many leadership capacities while at Coffee, including the demanding job of yearbook editor during her senior year. Academically strong at each level, Michelle excelled in the classroom at Coffee and later at UNA. She was named Woman of the Year at UNA in 1996, which was one among the many awards she received while in college.

"My time at Coffee and UNA are among the best memories of my life," said Michelle. "I remain involved by serving on the CHS Alumni Scholarship Board and on the UNA Alumni Board. While Coffee is no longer, after the consolidation of both high schools into Florence High School in 2004, the memories are dear and close to my heart."

While reflecting on her memories at UNA, Michelle's husband, Jeff, ever so slowly entered the conversation.

"The first time I laid eyes on Michelle in 1995, I said to a friend, 'I'm going to marry that girl'," Jeff said. "She didn't know I existed at this time, but I remember what she was wearing down to her Birkenstock sandals. As fate would have it, we met a year later, and my vision proved correct as we married three years later in 1998."

After graduating with an English and professional writing degree from UNA, Michelle moved to Starkville, Mississippi, to complete her Master's degree. Michelle began exploring job opportunities after this experience and was hired by the TimesDaily in Florence.

"I like to say I came to be a journalist through the back door," Michelle said. "The job I was hired to do was at the copy desk as a copy editor. An opening later came up in the newsroom, and I wasn't the first choice. But as it turned out, the individual who was initially selected decided to accept employment elsewhere. The reporter job was offered to me, and thus began my journalism career. I loved working as a reporter."

As a journalist for the TimesDaily, Michelle garnered national recognition when she received the highly-acclaimed Wilbur Award in 2008. The Religion Communicators Council, or RCC, presents these awards to promote and encourage excellence in the communication of religious faith through a variety of secular media. The Wilbur Award, first given in 1949, honors Marvin C. Wilbur, a pioneer in the field of religious public relations. Michelle's winning piece was entitled the "Front Lines of Faith."

"As part of the research, I visited a number of religious ceremonies – from the initiation of a Buddhist into the temple to a baptism in a Southern Baptist Church. It was wonderful as well as enlightening to be a part of so many faith-based experiences," said Michelle. "One thing each has in common is the 'do unto others as you would have them do onto you' theme."

After a satisfying thirteen years with the TimesDaily, Michelle made a career change in 2011. Michelle is a natural leader who has a rare ability to analyze complex issues and then make informed decisions. Additionally, she employs her highly effective communications skills in her current role as the Director of Community Relations for Shoals Hospital.

"I will always be a writer," said Michelle. "But the weekend work didn't allow me to enjoy time with my family. My family is my life. My husband, Jeff, is my superstar, and my daughters, Maeve and Ally, bless me every day. My job for the hospital allows me to do the fun stuff, and I work with outstanding people. I plan and organize events and handle all of the media relations."

In addition to working full-time, being a wife and mother, Michelle is passionately involved in community service. She works with Downtown Florence Unlimited, or DFU, First Fridays, and the Florence Bicentennial Committee. She and her husband have recently completed the first of two years as chairpersons for Arts Alive, a well-known festival that draws thousands of people to Wilson Park in downtown Florence each May.

"This festival has a special significance," said Michelle. "My first official date with Jeff was to Arts Alive in May of 1997. In March of 1998, we were married. Jeff and I went to the Lauderdale County Courthouse on our lunch breaks for the ceremony. I'm pretty sure I wore pants. Instead of the traditional wedding, we enjoyed a two-week honeymoon in Europe – Paris, London, Belgium, and Amsterdam. It was wonderful."

It became obvious Michelle embraces everything about the art world with deep passion.

"You are correct," said Michelle. "I dearly love the arts, and I gave Jeff a folk art piece for Christmas years ago, and he was hooked as well. Jeff now knows the folk art world better than I do. We travel to art shows, and the artists have become our friends. Our home is filled with interesting pieces that tell fascinating stories."

Michelle seldom slows down to recharge her batteries. But she has learned a serious lesson about what's important. A few years ago, she took a 365-day hiatus from purchasing items for herself.

"I read about a woman who did this and decided to see if I could as well," said Michelle. "I only bought what I could eat or deplete. I learned not to be so materialistic. I started to give and give and give. We really don't need all of that stuff. Material possessions do not fill the hunger inside for a sense of fulfillment and wonder. Maybe I should do it again. Will you join me?"

Michelle exudes a positive demeanor, but we all face difficult struggles. For her, one of the toughest struggles was the tragic and sudden death of her older sister, Amy.

"It was and still is the toughest time in my life," Michelle said. "I had to get help because my life was falling apart – my marriage, my career, my ability to parent our daughter, Maeve, who wasn't quite two at the time. Counseling and faith got me through it—still gets me through, at times, and I learned one of the most valuable lessons, one that has stuck with me. I learned that I could break apart or break open. I chose the latter, and it's made all the difference."

Of course, that doesn't mean there aren't still bad days, so what's her coping mechanism?

"I indulge in a good cry," she said, "Get it out. Many consider this a weakness, but I think it's necessary. We are more blessed than ninety percent of the people in the world, but it can be difficult to see the blessings when confronting grief. As a family, we tell one another that we will get through this."

Eubanks spoke about taking some time, even ten minutes, to slow down and breathe in this fast-paced and stress-filled world.

"We should take a deep breath," said Michelle. "It's crucial for us to then regroup and move forward with clarity and purpose."

It became clear that faith and family formed a solid foundation upon which Michelle's life has been centered.

"My family is my life," she said. "I count my blessings every day. I am certain that God is in control of my ultimate destination. My daughters and my husband are the heart and soul of my life. "

Michelle's dear friend, Lexi Sandlin, spoke about the characteristics that define Michelle Eubanks.

"Michelle is positive; she exudes happiness, confidence, and contentment," said Lexi. "She could be having the worst day of her life, and you wouldn't know it. She is skilled at getting information that will enable those with whom she interacts to make fair decisions. She's the perfect choice to chair Arts Alive."

Michelle has seen firsthand the lifestyles afforded to residents in large cities and smaller communities through her travels. Why does she choose to live here?

"I first came back because it was easy," Michelle said. "Jeff had a job, and we had family here. But as we've grown, I've realized it's the perfect size for us and the lives we want to lead. A smaller town would not give us the amenities and sense of community or the friends, and a larger city would take all of that away. I feel safe here with our children, and they are getting a sound education. If there was a problem in this area, I feel like I could reach out and get help. We're fortunate to have a support network in Florence. You don't realize how important this is until you travel somewhere and come back. We then know why we live here and call this home."

Would you encourage others to get involved in their community as volunteers?

"Absolutely," said Michelle. "If you love where you live, why not learn, give, and do things to make it better. I've found that, by giving of my time, I can be a part of something much bigger than myself and possibly make contributions that have long-term and lasting effects. When it's all said and done, if someone comes to visit your town, they might be tempted to stay by saying, 'This is a pretty neat place to live.' How humbling is that to be a part of something that can impact people's lives."

Does it bother you that many young people leave home for the larger cities after graduation?

"Many graduating students leave for jobs and all the stuff," Michelle said. "I could have left, like others, but chose to stay because I believed in the community. I wanted to help make this area better so that my children one day could call this home. But you have to want to stay. This is true in any town across the country. It's the people who want to stay who make a difference for future generations."

The 2015 Arts Alive Festival recently concluded, and, by all accounts, it was a resounding success. In fact, many people were overheard describing this year's event as the best in its twenty-nine year history. What might account for this? Might it have something to do with the chairwoman's deep love and appreciation for the artists in the folk art world? Doesn't passion for something create a tasty recipe for success? The answer seems obvious. The final words are left to Michelle.

"I believe it does," said Michelle. "I know my heart is in the right place because I dearly love the arts, but this is about We, not I. If my passion inspires others to serve, then I am honored and humbled. I believe in leading by example. There is nothing I won't do to help out. If not, this would be considered bossing, not leading.

"My primary goal is to bring attention to the events, such as First Fridays, Arts Alive, or our fabulous university, the University of North Alabama. By offering our time, together, we can enhance the organizations and improve the community in which we live. By doing so, others, perhaps even our children, will take notice, and get involved. It's about committing time and energy to leave our town better than we found it. If we are motivated by passion for the things we love, the sky is the limit. I look forward to working side-by-side with you as we pitch in to make our already magical area known as the Shoals an even better place to call home."

Chapter 24

Tom Braly

Tom Braly's daily activities were motived by honesty, fair play, and the sound principles of Christian living. His associates in the field of athletics recognized his ability, his honesty, and his sense of justice and fairness. The people who came under the guiding hand of Tom Braly found their lives greatly enriched by the experience. The teacher in him believed in firm discipline but only when it was delivered with a friendly dose of encouraging advice. Tom believed that empowering others was the best way to establish trust and gain strong performances from fellow employees. When he observed mistakes, instead of being critical, Tom was kind, encouraging, and understanding. These are the reasons he is featured in this book.

A cool rain was falling on this late summer afternoon when I pulled into the driveway of Brenda Braly Spears, daughter of Tom Braly. Although Mr. Braly has been gone for more than fifty years, I could envision him answering the door and saying: "Bill, this sure is a beautiful day. Don't you love these cool rainy days when football season is around the corner?"

It was the simple things in life that produced the most joy for the humble man who taught history, coached all sports, and served as principal for the former Coffee High School in Florence, Alabama.

Tom Braly Jr., was born in 1913, the second child of five to Thomas Madden Braly Sr., and Ethel Pearl Braly, of Russellville, Alabama. The elder Tom Braly supported the family by working as a quarry foreman for Sloss-Sheffield Mining Company, now Vulcan Materials. Tom was raised in a loving home and regularly attended First United Methodist Church in Russellville.

Shortly after he was born, a nickname, Buddy, was assigned to him, and this would remain his moniker for the remainder of his life.

"His brother, Roy, was three-years-old when Dad was born," said Brenda. "My grandmother told me that Roy glanced at the baby and said, 'Well, that's my little buddy.' The brothers became dear friends, and, when dad started to walk, Roy would always tell his friends about his little buddy."

Tom developed another close friend in Russellville, Walton Wright, and the two boys were inseparable during high school and college. They were teammates on the baseball, football, and basketball teams while at Russellville High School and later as athletes at Birmingham-Southern College.

"Dad graduated from high school at sixteen as the salutatorian of his class," said Brenda. "He was awarded an academic and athletic scholarship to Birmingham-Southern College in Birmingham. Dad followed his friend, Walton, to Birmingham-Southern. Despite playing three sports in college, both men also played semi-pro baseball during the summers to earn extra money. I vividly remember them talking about playing for the cotton mill towns."

Tom and Walton were both members of First United Methodist Church in Russellville. They did everything together and both later became teachers, coaches, and an inspiration to many people. Football stadiums are named in their honor. Braly Municipal Stadium, home to the University of North Alabama Lions and the Florence Falcons, was named in Mr. Braly's honor in 1964. The Sheffield Bulldogs, where Walton Wright coached football for twenty-eight years, named its field in his honor in 1999.

"Dad would be embarrassed by the attention," said Brenda. "But he loved that stadium and the games on Friday evenings. He also loved Saturday mornings when he took my brother and his friends to play on the field. Dad loved everything about Coffee High School – the teachers, the kids, and all of the workers behind the scenes."

In addition to being a standout athlete at Birmingham-Southern, Braly was elected to Omicron Delta Kappa during his senior year in 1936. ODK is a national leadership honor society that was founded in 1914 at Washington and Lee University in Lexington, Virginia. ODK was the highest honor that could be bestowed upon a young man at the time at Birmingham-Southern College. Tom was also elected president of his senior class at Southern in 1935-1936.

"Dad was hired by Lauderdale County in 1936, and his first assignment was to teach and coach every sport at Waterloo High School," said Brenda. "I have the letter that relates his salary, which included coaching responsibilities, to be one-hundred dollars per month."

While at Waterloo, the principal called the newly hired coach into his office and told him that his responsibilities would include paddling the students who misbehaved.

"My dad said, 'I can't do that'," Brenda said. "Dad didn't condone paddling students and never did so. He believed in meeting with the students first, and, if unsuccessful, he would then involve the parents."

Mr. Braly left Waterloo after a year to take on the same duties at Hackleburg High School. It was the next summer, in 1938, when Tom Braly first met the girl who would become the love of his life.

"Dad was coaching summer baseball in nearby Haleyville when he first laid eyes on my mom, Sybil Barber," Brenda said. "Mom's hometown was Haleyville, and she happened to see Dad at the ball field. They began dating and were married a year and a half later, in 1940. Many will remember mom from her teaching days at Powell Elementary School."

Mr. Braly and his new bride were at Marion County High School in Guin, Alabama when Tom got the call that his services were requested as a history teacher and coach for football, basketball, and baseball at Coffee High School in Florence, Alabama, in 1941.

Once Tom and Sybil were settled in Florence, they had two children, Brenda Braly Spears and the late Tom Braly III. Mr. Braly loved being a father, Brenda said.

As at school, Tom Braly was a gentle spirit at home. Brenda fondly recalled her mom sharing stories about the couple dancing at home to the music provided by a classic 1939 Stromberg-Carlson Console Radio. Brenda's mom also told her that her dad listened nightly to this radio for updates concerning World War II events.

"Dad picked up war news on the radio," Brenda recalled her mom telling her. "He shared any news updates the following day with students and the community in the Coffee auditorium. He also shared the dreadful news if he was informed of a local man being killed in action."

As a testament to his role at Coffee, the senior class in 1945 dedicated its Coffee Pot yearbook to then-coach Tom Braly.

"The students said that he inspired them through his sympathetic understanding of their problems," said Brenda. "Dad had been with this class all four years, and the students spoke of his high standards of character. This was the twenty-fifth edition of the Coffee Pot. Many former players and students have shared with me how Dad showed a special interest in them. I'm not surprised because Daddy was a deeply compassionate man."

In 1946, Coach Braly was promoted to principal at Coffee High School and served in that capacity until 1963.

"Dad was humbled by the honor to serve as principal," said Brenda. "However, he made it vividly clear that he was always a teacher first. He believed that his job was to guide, lead, and help everyone working under his supervision. I recall him saying, 'The best thing I can do for a good teacher is to leave him or her alone'."

Brenda still has vivid memories of one particular day at school when her Dad was in charge at CHS.

"It was late November in 1963, and I was in Hot Linville's class," she said. "Dad's calm but reassuring voice came on the intercom. It was quiet because rumors were floating. Dad said, 'Our President has died. Please say a silent prayer.' He then said, 'Proceed to the auditorium, and I will tell you all I know.' He delivered the tragic news that President Kennedy had, indeed, been assassinated. All I remember is tears, hugs, and simply being there for one another."

Exactly eight days later, the Braly family was enjoying a wonderful day at Legion Field in Birmingham on November 30, 1963, for the Iron Bowl, the classic Southern rivalry between Alabama and Auburn. Auburn, led by coach Ralph "Shug" Jordan, defeated Bear Bryant and the Tide in a nail-biter by a score of 10-8.

"Daddy wasn't feeling well on the ride home," said Brenda. "We were stopped for a tail-light infraction by a state patrolman on Highway 43, just before reaching Russellville. We were on 43 because Daddy insisted that we visit his mom whenever we were near Russellville. Daddy seemed calm and was chatting with the trooper. He was not arrested, but the trooper asked him to come back into the patrol car. While Daddy was in the patrol car, a second patrolman, who was also in the car, came to see Mom and said, 'Does your husband have epilepsy'? Mom shouted, 'No, but he could be having a heart attack! Please get us to the hospital and call his brother, Roy, an agent for the Alabama Beverage Control, in Russellville.'

"I jumped into the patrol car along with mom, and we sat on each side of Daddy in the back seat," said Brenda. "Mom said, 'Brenda, put his nitro pills under his tongue.' I did so as the trooper sped to the Russellville hospital. The other trooper drove our car and my brother to the hospital. Uncle Roy was waiting for us, and he picked up his Little Buddy and carried him over his shoulder into the emergency room. I don't know how Uncle Roy did this, but we were too late. Daddy passed away at the age of fifty in the same town that he was raised."

After receiving the tragic news of their father's passing, the family of three returned to their home in Edgemont in Florence.

"It was around eleven in the evening, and our house was full of people," said Brenda. "The first person we saw was Hot Linville, a close friend. Everyone was there to offer love and support at this sad time. These folks dearly loved my Daddy, and they were so comforting."

When someone leaves us too soon, it seems important to reflect on what matters in the grand scheme of things, the big picture if you will. What is the precise measurement for a successful and meaningful life? Tom Braly believed that his purpose in life was to inspire others to lead honorable and Christian lives of meaning. By using his God-given abilities, Tom was able to make a remarkable difference in the lives of many people. And as his daughter will attest, he enjoyed every day of his life along the way.

"Daddy's calling was to help people," Brenda said. "That's why he became a teacher. He loved visiting with former students and hearing about their lives. Daddy would rather visit with a long-lost friend than take an all-expenses paid vacation to Hawaii. That's who he was: a man who loved people and a man who appreciated the accomplishments of others. I believe that Daddy helped somebody every single day in his life. By doing so, I'm convinced that he was the most contented person I've ever known."

Chapter 25

Charlotte Tomlinson Homan

*E*motional strength is the ability to handle an unforeseen turn of events and remain balanced and calm. Charlotte Tomlinson Homan developed this quality early in her life as the eldest of six children growing up in Coffeeville, Alabama, to Ray and Mary Benson Tomlinson. Her father was a craftsman, a mason builder, and her mother taught English for more than forty years. Charlotte knows that our histories are determined by the individual choices we make. So in making any life-changing decisions, she always prayed for the ability to think deeply and clearly, and for God's strength to keep her in touch with her system of values. During her fascinating life, Charlotte has also learned that it's the small things in life that really matter. She is featured here to remind us of this important lesson.

Charlotte lived in a small country community, twenty-five miles from the nearest doctor. Her maternal grandmother, Mrs. Odie Benson, was the matriarch of the area where most everyone loved and supported one another.

"When it was time for me to enroll in first grade, my mother was just days away from giving birth to a sibling," said Charlotte. "She could not accompany me, so I picked up my satchel and walked over a mile to school! It felt perfectly normal in the small first-through 12th grade school I attended."

Her father developed tuberculosis while working on a construction project in Texas when Charlotte was in the third grade. Charlotte, her two siblings, and her mother moved in with Grandmother Benson.

"My Daddy was required to go to a special sanatorium in Montgomery," Charlotte said. "We could only visit him by peering through a screened porch looking in from the outside. Thankfully, we remained healthy, and he came home a year later. That year of 1956 was life-changing. Daddy's first agenda item was to give his life to Christ in a small Baptist church with his nine-year old daughter walking the aisle behind him. He and I were baptized to-gether in the Tombigbee River."

Several years earlier, before Charlotte was school-aged, her Dad was away for stretches of time playing semi-pro baseball. Since her mother accompanied her Dad on these base-ball trips, Charlotte stayed with a nanny named Pearlie.

"Pearlie was in her sixties, a widow, and had one child who was a teacher," Charlotte said. "I lived with Pearlie in her small immaculate home for extended periods. The lon-ger I was with her, the more I thought I belonged to her. I slept with her at night in a bed weighted down with heavy old quilts. The pot-bellied stove kept us warm when it was cold."

Pearlie's influence on Charlotte was unmistakable.

"A normal breakfast for us was pot liquor from last night's turnip greens and soda crack-ers to top it off," said Charlotte. "In the late afternoon, we raked the dirt yard to make it clean and cared for. I danced in the yard smelling sweet buds from shrubs and flowers. We sat on the porch and watched the sun go down. It was a beautiful way to see the world. It was love translated into its simplistic form. She loved me, and I loved her – nothing else mattered."

When Charlotte was older, she spent time shadowing her grandmother, Miss Odie. Her grandfather, the Post Master of Coffeeville, died tragically and left her thirty-five-year-old grandmother to raise five small children.

"Odie Mae Benson was determined, creative, and innovative," said Charlotte. "Miss Odie used her assets and talents to open a boarding house and a small café, and she built small primitive cabins for hunters and fishermen drawn to the area known as the Tombigbee Paradise. I worked beside my grandmother waiting tables, washing dishes, and working the cash register. I remember the back room in her café for colored people. She loved them, served them, and always treated them with respect. I grew up working side-by-side in the kitchen with the hired help."

Some valuable life lessons were imparted to Charlotte by her grandmother.

"Miss Odie worked from dawn until closing time," said Charlotte. "She never complained and gave God the glory for each day. No one ever drifted too low or lost their way so that she couldn't lift them up. She would take them to the foot of the cross, as it was, and promise that she and her sweet Jesus would see them through their problem. She taught me that good food and love could cure about anything. I learned that hard work is honorable, that you should be willing to help those less fortunate, to count your blessings, and trust the Lord to hold you in the palm of his hand."

It was not unusual to see a few state dignitaries visit Miss Odie in Coffeeville.

"I remember seeing three governors of Alabama visit her personally," Charlotte said. "They were Big Jim Folsom, Albert Brewer, and George Wallace. They sought my grandmother's wise advice."

Charlotte always believed that she would attend college on the plains at Auburn University. However, a serious high school boyfriend changed that, and she followed him to the University of Alabama in Tuscaloosa.

"My boyfriend and I lasted six months after I began my college career," said Charlotte. "But this allowed me to meet my future husband, Dennis Homan. Once Dennis and I began dating, the rest was history. Dennis played football for the Crimson Tide and his coach, Paul Bryant, supported the union. We married in January of 1968 before Dennis obtained his degree and left soon thereafter for Dallas, Texas."

Coach Bryant stayed close to the Homans and their children until his death in 1983.

"He sent me flowers when Matt and Missy were born, and he and Mary Harmon loved to have us come to their home and visit them in Tuscaloosa," Charlotte said.

A good friend of the Homan's, Ray Perkins, shared a few thoughts about the couple who recently celebrated their forty-seventh wedding anniversary.

"Dennis held the touchdown reception record at Alabama for forty-seven years until Amari Cooper broke it in the 2014 season," Ray said. "But Dennis's best catch while playing for Coach Bryant was Charlotte. They're a great couple."

The Homan family lived in Dallas, Kansas City, Missouri, Tuscaloosa, and Birmingham during the next eight years as Dennis played football in the NFL and the World Football League. After football, the family relocated to Florence in 1976 when Dennis began a second career as a drug representative with Abbott Labs.

"The size of this small community was surprising at the time," said Charlotte. "But, over the years, it has truly become home. Our daughter, Missy Homan, lives here with our precious twin grandchildren, Hannah and Kneeland Hibbett. Our son, Matt lives in nearby Athens with his wife, Jill, and their two children, Sydney and Reid."

Dale Tomlinson, the second oldest of the children behind Charlotte, said of her sister: "Even now, I seek Charlotte's counsel with confidence because I know her life's journey has given her a deep well of wisdom and insight few others have. I am blessed beyond measure to call her sister."

After a year of getting settled in Florence, Charlotte enrolled at the University of North Alabama in 1977 to pursue a Bachelor's of Science degree in Nursing. Charlotte graduated summa cum laude in 1980 and maintained a perfect 4.0 grade point average. She has remained active with the UNA nursing program and is a charter member of the UNA nursing honor society. Her nursing and management career spanned more than twenty-five years.

The list of honors and recognitions are too numerous to mention, and she says that's not what it was about anyway. Her plaques are in the attic.

"My decision to return to college was to support family goals," said Charlotte. "We pitched in with chores and responsibilities together. I can remember studying anatomy and chemistry at baseball games and gymnastic events. Dennis and the children contributed in ways that made all of us stronger individually and as a team."

The most rewarding days in Charlotte's nursing career were at the bedside or in the homes of her patients. Management aspirations and administrative roles were never in her plans, Charlotte said.

"However, the management positions that came to me seemed to fit my skill sets at the time," said Charlotte. "It felt good to take struggling programs and pull the staff and medical community together to improve services and patient care. I often spoke to community clubs, universities, and professional organizations on health-or service-related topics. As a Director of Nursing, I always felt nursing the nurse would allow them to work in the best environment to offer quality care for our patients. Nursing is forever about caring for others."

Charlotte has learned to search for the good that can come from loss and sadness.

"Life is full of loss," Charlotte said. "I have learned from personal pain and disappointment in people who have betrayed me. But I've learned to let the Lord make it right. I've learned to train my heart to listen for the lessons during life's darkest times. It is better to be kind than to be right. Go to a trusted friend and seek wise counsel. It is important to have those who can support and encourage us. We can make it easier by being strong together with words of hope and healing."

Charlotte believes that many people focus their time on unimportant matters and insignificant relationships.

"Life is too short to play pretend," said Charlotte. "You and only you know who truly loves you. These are the people you should embrace with every fiber of your heart and soul. I believe that genuine friendship is a partnership of the best kind. It's not a matter of quantity, but of lasting quality and loyalty. The best gift is to give of your time to someone or some important endeavor – then you are truly investing yourself."

A dear friend, Debbie Guy, shared a few thoughts about Charlotte. The two have been like sisters and have tackled life's big and small problems since they met in 1976.

"Charlotte extends her family to include those in need," she said. "Charlotte lights up any room with an inner beauty that is filled with her belief in Christ. She is never too busy to listen, care, or to help. She offers support, comfort, and strength when it's most needed. I think Charlotte is one of God's special chosen people. She is sweet and sensitive to all of the people around her. She is the greatest friend of all."

It is important to realize that any good deeds performed do not have an expiration date.

"I believe that with my heart and soul," said Charlotte. "The good we do is not limited by time but will live on through many lifetimes to come. All of our deeds, our choices, and our witness touch others by inspiring, healing, and changing. Many who are influenced by our actions are beyond our own awareness. God puts us where we are for a purpose."

Marie Lewey, Charlotte's sister, spoke about the impact the eldest sibling has played in the lives of all six of the Tomlinson children.

"Our big sister Charlotte played a key role in all of our lives," Marie said. "She's the oldest, so for me, the baby girl, she was like a 'sister mom' – nurturing, instructive, and full of wisdom. This remains her special role to this day. Even today, there are often 'call Charlotte' moments. She always knows what to do, and she's still taking care of her siblings with love and devotion."

Charlotte believes that all of us need a special place we can go when our lives are in need of re-examination and balance.

"Find your place," said Charlotte. "For me, it's the beach. This should allow you to renew and balance your spirit. Your place should inspire deep reflection and refresh your spirit. This is necessary for emotional healing and a new vision for the future."

Charlotte is a strong individual formed by blessings and challenges that have shaped her into the unique woman she is today. She knows that it's the small things in life that really matter, such as having lunch with a dear friend, a random act of kindness, or time with the grandkids. Charlotte's favorite Bible verse is Philippians 4:13. It reads: I can do all things through Christ who gives me strength.

"I have and do believe that verse with all my heart," said Charlotte. "I am convinced that God has given me angels to guide, teach, and protect me since birth. This is my story. I'm positive that I have been surrounded with God's presence as long as I have lived. And lastly, we should remember that in the final analysis, when it's our time to go, it is the investment of friendships, time, energy, and benevolence we planted and left behind that really matters."

Chapter 26

Allen Tomlinson

$\mathcal{A}$llen Tomlinson has been in the advertising and public relations business throughout his professional life, which spans a remarkable thirty-five years. To succeed in this business, one must have the ability to shape opinions. Allen was doing a masterful job at this, but, at some point in his mid-thirties, he realized it was taking a lot of energy selling the world on the fact that he was straight, because he wasn't. He realized the most important thing for him was to be honest with the world, and, in doing so, a huge burden was lifted. Allen soon discovered there are people who loved, respected, and supported him, regardless of his sexual orientation. Allen is included because of the courage with which he lives his life.

Among Allen's already impressive skills set is his pleasing and confident tone of voice. While he seems embarrassed by the observation, it's clear that he has mastered the art of verbal communication.

"I'm the oldest of three children from Cherokee, Alabama," said Allen. "I suppose my people skills come to me naturally because of Mom and Dad. My dad, Charles, was a graduate of Sewanee University, and my mom, Susanna, was the second woman to graduate with a degree in chemical engineering from the University of Alabama in 1955."

Allen described his early years of growing up in a small rural community as being enjoyable and comfortable. His father was a forester, and his mom commuted to the Tennessee Valley Authority to work as a chemical engineer. While Allen's brother followed his dad his into forestry, this was never a consideration for Allen. Allen always knew his career would involve something that included interacting with people. This seemed to come naturally to him because his parents were both outstanding communicators.

"My dad was well-known for his storytelling talents," said Allen. "Mom was a natural communicator in her own right, and they beautifully complimented each other. Following my parents retirements, their greatest joy was found in travelling the world, often with family and friends. However, Mom remained active with the Cherokee Library Friends and with the Tennessee Valley Art Association. My love for travelling comes from them."

Allen said he was blessed to be close to his grandparents, Bob and Eloise Martin Tomlinson. Bob attended and graduated from Whittier College, a private liberal arts school, in Whittier, California.

"My granddad was a cheerleader at Whittier," said Allen. "He spoke frequently about his assistant, the kid who carried his equipment, and that kid was Richard Nixon. The Nixon and Tomlinson families were close friends, and Granddad stayed in touch with Nixon over the years. I recall him saying that he couldn't believe the young Nixon he knew was capable of such behavior in the Watergate scandal in 1973."

Bob Tomlinson met Eloise while both were students at Whittier.

"My granddad followed my grandmother back to Florence, Alabama," Allen said. "Grandmother grew up on Park Boulevard in Sheffield in the house now owned by Mac McAnally, the American country music singer-songwriter. I'm not certain, but I suspect my grandparents were married in First Methodist Church in Sheffield, Alabama. Granddad was a Quaker and Grandmother was a Methodist; they became Episcopalians after they married."

Allen's family attended Trinity Episcopal Church in Florence, and Allen's most vivid memories involve his Granddad Bob playing the piano and, occasionally, the organ at church.

"When it was time to leave Sunday school, Granddad was always playing the piano and his favorite song, 'Onward Christian Soldiers'," said Allen. "We kids marched in single-file out of our classes and into the chapel to Granddad's music. Most everyone my age or older who attended Trinity will remember this experience. My grandparents also hosted an annual Christmas 'Sing' at their home in Hickory Hills. We kids were given sheets of paper with the song lyrics, Granddad played the piano, and we sang and sang. The adults sang along as well. It was a special family time."

Is it possible that Allen is just as gifted at music as he is at advertising?

"I love music but am not an accomplished musician," Allen said. "I wish I had Granddad's talent because he always told me that playing the piano allowed him to attract people anywhere in the world. It was like an icebreaker, and people gravitated to him because of his talent."

Allen attended Cherokee High School in the small town of Cherokee, Alabama. He recalled his days in the tiny school as being wonderful.

"There were seventy-three of us in my senior class," Allen said. "But I would not have traded my high school experience for anything. The sad part about the small-town life, for parents, is that most kids leave for college and never return. These days, I think the typical graduating class at Cherokee is more like twenty students."

Allen went on to Auburn University where he graduated in 1980 with a degree in communications and journalism. Later that same year, he opened his own advertising business in Florence, Alabama. He also started a family and is the proud father of three children, Molly, Reed, and Caroline.

"I dearly love my children," said Allen. "I'm divorced from my first wife and met my partner, David Sims, in 1996. We've been together since, and David has been instrumental in helping with all the responsibilities of raising children. When the kids were fifteen, thirteen, and eleven, they came to live permanently with David and me."

Allen and David are very active in the lives of the children, all of whom are adults with college degrees and careers. Eldest daughter Molly, who lives in Washington D.C., spoke on behalf of all three children.

"My dad is the kindest man I know and the best father a girl could ask for," she said. "We feel similarly about David. He always keeps us laughing and is the perfect partner for

Dad. We feel lucky to have not one but two amazing fathers. They are the kindest, most generous, and hardest-working couple I know. Having a non-traditional family has taught us a lot about treating other people with respect. We're all human, and we're all loved by someone."

Allen and David not only raised the children together, but they also began and maintain a thriving business. They have been receiving rave reviews regarding their bi-monthly publication. In fact, the name change from A. Tomlinson/Sims Advertising to No'Ala Studios more coincides with everything the firm does as well as better reflects their partnership.

With work and home life so intertwined, is it difficult to find balance?

"David is the creative partner," said Allen. "I'm the writer in the business. Simply put, David is responsible for the way things look, the artwork, and the design. I'm the salesman and call on clients, advertisers, and potential new clients. Our talented staff of ten people is the best we have ever employed. They are incredible."

David's artwork has appeared in gallery shows, and many in the Shoals and beyond are familiar with the trio of pieces he did for Arts Alive, the annual arts show that takes place in May in Wilson Park. The most famous of the trio is the red dog, the first of the three. Allen said he's come to depend on David's creativity.

"David is really good," said Allen. "When he joined the firm in 1996, his graphic art skills made my job far easier. He's the best I've seen as a graphic artist."

Since coming out publicly as a gay man almost twenty years ago, Allen said he's learned to handle the criticism when it comes.

"This comes with age," he said. "Everyone is not going to like you, so why worry about something out of your control? We live honestly, and we are concerned with helping people instead of hurting them. I would like to think that I'm pretty good at shaping peoples' opinions because that's my business. However, in my early thirties, I had three kids and had gradually come to the realization of who I was. The most important thing to me was to be honest, and, upon doing so, it felt like a huge burden had been lifted. I got a divorce and began living the life I knew I was meant to live."

Many people, regardless of age, are hesitant to come out because they're afraid of the reactions of others, especially family and close friends. Allen said his parents made his decision to live honestly that much easier.

"My parents, unlike many, were totally supportive," said Allen. "David's parents were the same. Sadly, this is not the case when many people acknowledge they are gay. Many are kicked out by family members, disowned, and thrown out of their churches. David and I often lend our time to various organizations to help these individuals by assuring them that everything will be okay."

Despite living in what some would consider a small town, Allen said he believes Florence to be a creative community with a large population of artists.

"We're fortunate to live in Florence," said Allen. "To be creative, one must realize that not everyone thinks the way you do or lives the way you do, and these individuals have a higher tolerance of people who are different. This is a wonderful place to live."

Allen and David love to travel when time permits in their busy work schedules.

"We have clients in Washington D.C., and this makes for a special trip," said Allen. "We call on our clients and also get to visit with our daughter, Molly, who lives in D.C. It's the best of both worlds. The business world has changed, and this allows us to work for clients around the globe. We also have clients in Portland, Oregon. David and I have come to love that area as well, and we have developed fifteen or twenty close friends on the West Coast."

With so many years in the business, it's no wonder Allen, David, and No'Ala Studios have won so many awards.

"We have been fortunate to receive many awards," said Allen "We don't talk much about this, but our magazine has been honored with awards in just about every category."

Putting it all together – the career, the kids, the relationship – Allen Tomlinson has led a rich and deeply fulfilling life. He said he's learned from the good times and the bad.

"Sometimes, it becomes necessary to pick your family," Allen said. "There are people in the world that will love you, respect you, and support you, but it may not include your biological family. It's hard, really hard, but you have to reach a point in your life and say, 'This is who I am, and I'm a good person who treats others with compassion and dignity.' The world is different today and more accepting. I believe when you make the choice to live as you intended, you will find, like I did, that life becomes more enriching than you could possibly have imagined."

Chapter 27

Jane Silverman Frith

*J*ane Frith possesses an energy level that would be the envy of many world-class Olympic athletes. She moves quickly, speaks at a rapid clip, and she works tirelessly for the things in which she believes. Jane is so busy helping others that it's easy to forget about her lifelong passion for the visual arts and her genuine love and appreciation of history. She is included to encourage us to learn more about history and the artistic people who document their lives through their unique expression.

Jane is the only child of deceased parents Aaron "Silvo" and Irene Silverman of Mobile, Alabama. Her dad, although he passed away when Jane was just nine, was a huge influence in her life. According to his daughter, Silvo Silverman was known for his deep love of history and his genuine compassion for others.

"My dad was quite the student at the University of Alabama in the mid-1920s," said Jane. "He was a member of Jasons Honor Society, a society reserved for men who display qualities of academics, responsibility, and leadership. He was also in Omicron Delta Kappa, a national leadership honor society. After graduating in 1929 from the university, he lived in several places before moving to Mobile."

When Jane was eight, her father took her and her mom to New York City for a family celebration. While she was there, she was a participant in the Peanut Gallery on the "Howdy Doody Show." Jane even had her picture taken with the famous puppet. When she returned home, Jane said that she had become a minor celebrity in the neighborhood.

"Being on the 'Howdy Doody Show' in those days was a big deal," Jane said. "Also, the trip to New York was a milestone in my life. Because my dad loved history, we visited several historical places along the way. My dad's interest in history was infectious, and it kindled a love of history in me that still exists today."

Jane described her childhood as quintessentially American, not unlike that depicted in another classic TV Show, "Leave it to Beaver."

"I lived in a great neighborhood with lots of children," Jane said. "I could walk to the drug store, the grocery store, and to school. But in 1957, when I was nine years old, my dad passed away suddenly from a heart attack. This tragedy left Mom as the only widow in our neighborhood. It was simply devastating to lose him at such a young age."

How did your mom handle all of the responsibilities of raising a child at that time?

"Most of our friends attended the Springhill Avenue Temple, and they were deeply caring people of the Jewish faith," said Jane. "These friends rallied around us and helped us in all areas of our daily life. Our doctor never charged us a dime for my visits. The support by these friends was simply overwhelming. Even today, when reflecting on these years, I'm certain that by seeing our friends care and help, it instilled in me the same type of attitude to help others who are less fortunate. Mom worked as well as to support the two of us."

Because of such caring and supportive friends, Jane's very American childhood continued through high school even though there were hints of discrimination.

"I had wonderful teachers, especially, Georgine Bridgewater, my 11th grade history teacher," said Jane. "I kept her notes and used them when I later taught history. On the social side, it didn't really bother me that we Jewish girls were excluded from being members of high school sororities. That's the way it was. It's not that way anymore."

Jane graduated from Murphy High School in Mobile in 1966 and headed to the University of Alabama to begin her college education. Her parents had always stressed the importance of getting a good education, and it was assumed that Jane would get a college degree. She graduated with a Bachelor's of Science Degree in History and an English minor in 1970.

"It was really a good thing for me being from Mobile with a small Jewish population," Jane said. "I had a small number of Jewish friends at home, but this changed at the University of Alabama. I became a member of the Jewish sorority, Sigma Delta Tau, when beginning my freshman year at the university. I was suddenly around sorority sisters from all over the country. Also, because our sorority was small in number, I was encouraged by other members to become involved in sorority and campus activities. This was a great training ground and enhanced my self-confidence."

Jane's love of history prompted a sorority sister to suggest that she take an art history class.

"I was hooked," said Jane. "I took three different classes while at the university. I acquired a passion for art that still exists today. I developed a sort of mental bucket list of art and history. And I have been fortunate to travel in the United States and Europe to visit most of the places on my bucket list."

During her four years at Alabama, Jane excelled academically. She was inducted into the Mortar Board Honor Society her senior year in 1970. Mortar Board is the premier national honor society recognizing college seniors for superior achievement in scholarship, leadership, and service. Only a select few students on campus are invited to join this esteemed organization.

After graduation, Jane secured a teaching position at Tuscaloosa Junior High School.

"I had my last exam at the university on Saturday and began teaching on Tuesday morning," Jane said. "Talk about culture shock."

By this time, she and boyfriend, Tom Frith, had become a serious item. In fact, she and Tom were married later this same year in 1970. The newlyweds eventually moved to Nashville when Tom accepted a job as a salesman for McKesson Pharmaceuticals. When the Florence, Alabama, territory came available in 1974, they transferred to the area and have lived in the Shoals since. Tom and Jane recently celebrated their forty-forth wedding anniversary.

"We have loved living and raising our family in Florence," said Jane. "Our son, Andy, and his family live here and love it. Our daughter, Jennifer, lives not too far away in Atlanta.

We raised our children at First Presbyterian Church in Florence. I love this church and have learned extensively in Sunday school and Bible study. But while Tom and the kids are members, I have never converted from my Jewish faith, and I'm certain that I never will."

Jane was a stay-at-home mom during the formative years of her children's lives. But the title didn't exactly fit because there was always somewhere to be and something to do for the kids. In the mid-1990s, Jane taught history in the Florence City School System and then at Riverhill School, a private grade school founded in 1980.

"I enjoyed my years of teaching history and hoped that I was making a difference in the lives of those I taught," said Jane. "For me, learning has been a lifelong endeavor. That was the most important lesson I tried to impart to my students. At Riverhill, my students had to write the Socratic quote on every paper that read: The unexamined life is not worth living."

A former student and now friend of Jane's, Amanda Terry, said she enjoyed Mrs. Frith's class immensely.

"I was impressed with her knowledge and her encouraging spirit," said Amanda. "Jane Frith is truly a caring person who makes everyone she encounters feel special."

Jane is a two-time cancer survivor, but she doesn't let the disease or the fight with it define her. Instead, she's pursued new interests and fulfills her lifelong passions.

In the late 1990s, a chance weekend trip with close friends to the Kentuck Festival of the Arts in Northport, Alabama, made an enduring impression on her. She was immediately taken by the artwork and, perhaps more importantly, by the cast of characters who produced the pieces.

"I got hooked on folk art, and my husband has come to love it as well," said Jane. "We began visiting artists at their homes, bought art, and developed lasting friendships. There are too many to name, but Chris Clark, a well-known artist from Birmingham, became a dear friend. While Chris passed away a couple of years ago, we can still feel his zest for life in the art that he created."

Jane was so enamored with folk art that she and Stan Larkin began hosting an annual event at her home to sell her friends' pieces.

"Stan was an incredible person," said Jane. "We simply loved one another. He passed away several years ago, and it devastated me and my family. He was family. I'm so blessed to have many friends, but Stan Larkin was truly special. Hardly a day goes by that I don't think about him."

The annual sale no longer takes place, but Jane's love of folk art persists.

"It's not really about the piece of art but the story and the person behind the piece," said Jane. "These fascinating men and women are producing a piece of their heart. It's emotionally powerful. Every time I glance at one of my pieces of folk art, I'm reminded of my friends and the incredible story that inspired them to action. This passion has enriched my life beyond words. I talk frequently by phone to these artists and will always be blessed by their talents but even more by their genuine friendship."

With so many dear and genuine friendships, is there a special magic that Jane possesses that allows for such relationships? Her husband, Tom, instantly provided the answer.

"To have friends, you have to be a friend," said Tom. "My wife is as devoted to her friends as anyone I know. She doesn't have time for petty jealousies, cliques, or anything that promotes exclusion. She embraces everyone, and Jane doesn't have a phony bone in her body. I'm blessed to have many friends, but Jane is my best friend. Jane deeply cares for the friends in her life."

With so much to keep her busy in her life, Jane says she's not sure why she doesn't slow down.

"I just really don't know," Jane said. "I do love working the soup kitchen at First Presbyterian Church in downtown Florence, love helping people, and enjoy down-to-earth individuals and their stories. That's the best I can offer."

Jane Frith has led a fascinating and deeply fulfilling life overflowing with an abundance of lasting friendships.

"One thing I've found is that it's important to be open to new experiences and new friendships," Jane said. "By doing so, you might discover and develop lasting friendships in the most unexpected places. I'm living proof of this. My life has been forever enriched by meeting and becoming friends with the creative spirits in the world of folk art. Keep your eyes and ears open because you never know when someone will touch your heart in a manner that changes your life forever."

Since this chapter was written, Jane Frith suffered debilitating and life-altering injuries in an automobile accident on May 13, 2015. This leads us to ponder: Why do bad things happen to good people? In his best-selling book, "When Bad Things Happen to Good People," Rabbi Harold S. Kushner writes, "Let me suggest that the bad things that happen to us in our lives do not have meaning when they happen to us."

Rabbi Kushner goes on to suggest this is an unanswerable question, a pointless question. The Rabbi suggests a better question would be: "Since this has happened to me, what am I going to do about it?"

When suffering comes, and it comes to all of us at some point in our lives, our capacity for strength and love is put to a stern test. Jane and her family are facing this in the coming weeks, months and years. But one fact is unmistakably clear: They will not be facing these issues alone. Thousands of friends from all walks of life have displayed an outpouring of love along with a pledge to help and support the family during the difficult recovery period.

Jane Frith radiates an authenticity that is deeply rooted in her family, her friends, and her faith. She finds joy by seeing and embracing the joy of others. While she would be embarrassed by the observation, Jane is a rare individual. Why is this you might ask? It's because Jane cares; she cares about others and their personal life issues and concerns. Now it's time to turn the table, and let's care and support the person who has been there for us. We love you, Jane.

Chris Bobo

Chris Bobo dreamed of becoming a pilot as a young man growing up in Florence, Alabama. His dream came to fruition when he was commissioned as a second lieutenant in the United States Army in 1985, following his ROTC training at the University of North Alabama. Chris's first assignment in the United States Army was at Fort Rucker, Alabama, where he trained to become a helicopter pilot. Chris would go on to pilot helicopters for a combined fourteen years in the U.S. Army and the Mississippi National Guard. Although Chris loved the Army, he opted to return to Florence to join his dad in business and begin raising a family. He is included here to share some valuable lessons learned from his military experience about leadership and life.

Chris is the middle child of three to Scotty and Kathy Springer Bobo, of Florence, Alabama. Scotty was stationed in Fort Campbell, Kentucky, in 1971 when he elected to forgo a career in the Army; he opted, instead, to relocate the family of five to Florence. Scotty had grown up primarily in Florence, and this was also home to Chris's mom.

"I was beginning fourth grade when we moved to Florence," said Chris. "I attended Forest Hills Elementary School, Bradshaw High School, and then the University of North Alabama. I was baptized and confirmed in Trinity Episcopal Church in Florence and was an acolyte until I graduated from high school. In fact, I'm still an acolyte if someone is a no-show on Sunday. My two daughters were baptized and confirmed in this church. My mom, Kathy Bobo, has been a lifelong member, so I guess you could say Trinity is a special place for us."

Kathy Bobo said that her middle child was never one to sit still for very long. When he discovered scouting through the Boy Scouts, it was the perfect venue for his enthusiastic energy.

"Chris took to scouting right away," said Kathy. "My husband, Scotty, helped with the troop, and Chris attained the rank of Eagle Scout. He was the type who wanted to accomplish things. Becoming an Eagle Scout requires a lot of work, and Chris enjoyed the experience. There is no doubt that scouting taught him many valuable tools and life lessons."

Family, too, has always been important in Chris Bobo's life. His parents were outstanding role models, and Chris was blessed to be close to his grandparents and one great-grandparent. His maternal great-grandfather, Floyd Hill, lived to the ripe old age of one hundred and seven, and Chris recalls frequently having lunch with him while Chris was a student at UNA.

"We called him 'Bopy' (pronounced bop-pee)," said Chris. "I'm not sure where the nickname came from, but he was a deeply caring man. He loved to work in his garden, and you'd see him out there in the middle of summer, with a long-sleeved shirt on, hoeing like crazy. He lived alone and cared for himself until his one-hundredth birthday. Bopy lived near the UNA campus, and I would park at his house, and we'd have lunch all the time. He was an avid outdoorsman and hunter, and I learned a lot from him."

Scouting, growing up at Trinity, and his familial relationships all seemed to be building toward the next phase of Chris's life. After graduating from Bradshaw High School, Chris attended UNA on an ROTC scholarship. Reserve Officer Training Corps trains young men and women for active duty in the U.S. Army. While majoring in history at UNA, Chris excelled in the ROTC program and was a member of the inaugural UNA cross country team in 1984. This activity paid dividends for Chris, who would soon be facing rigorous fitness requirements in the U.S. Army.

Chris was selected Cadet Commander his senior year in 1984 and also named an Army ROTC Distinguished Military Graduate, an award based on scholarship, military aptitude, and leadership ability. This designation placed him in the top twenty percent of all Army ROTC graduates in the nation.

The George C. Marshall Award, given to one cadet per university, was awarded to Chris during his final year at the University of North Alabama. This award, named in memory of our 50th U.S. Secretary of State, is based on leadership, physical fitness, and community involvement.

"I was honored to receive this award," said Chris. "There were about two hundred and fifty of us nationwide chosen to go to Washington and Lee University for a four-day seminar. We rubbed shoulders with some top military leaders. We met the Secretary of Defense, Caspar Weinberger, and engaged in panel discussions about national defense. It was an incredible experience."

After graduation, the path was set for Chris's first assignment.

"I was sent to Fort Rucker, Alabama for aviation training," said Chris. "It was highly competitive to get into aviation, but my credentials from UNA secured me a slot. The training began sharply at four each morning. The instructor and I were seated side-by-side in a small TH 55 helicopter. I'll never forget the instructor's first words. He said, 'Well, start flying.' I had never flown, and learning how to hover – keeping the helicopter in the same place above the ground – was extremely difficult. Many new pilots couldn't master this, and, quite frankly, I had my doubts, but I finally succeeded. I was sent to Fort Campbell, Kentucky, after a year's training at Fort Rucker."

Chris met Jill Halderman while at Fort Campbell in 1989. She was a student at nearby Austin Peay State University in Clarksville, Tennessee, at the time. The pair hit it off immediately, and she had the honor of pinning his bars on when he was promoted to Captain in January of 1990. The couple married later that year at Trinity Episcopal Church in Clarksville, Tennessee.

"What are the odds?" Chris said. "Different churches but the same name."

Instead of accepting a solo assignment in Korea, however, the couple elected to relocate to Florence, Alabama, in 1992. Chris joined his dad in business but continued flying helicopters as part of the Mississippi National Guard in nearby Tupelo, Mississippi. Moving back to Florence and getting into the family business proved to have challenges of its own.

"Patience, understanding, and communication are the keys to success," Chris said. "I bought the business from Dad in 2000. He was – and still is – very supportive."

What, exactly, is the family business?

"Alabama Land Services," he said. "We're a land title company, which means we perform land title searches to certify that the seller in a real estate transaction owns the property. We then coordinate the transaction between buyer and seller and handle the financial distributions. Our company has been doing this since 1887. We like to say that, if you want it done right, you'll get it done right here."

His father helped prepare him to take over, Chris said, but so did his time in the military.

"I learned leadership skills in the Army," said Chris. "I believe the best environment for success is for your employees to want to follow you, instead of being made to follow you. Leadership by example was instilled in me during my stint in the Army, and I never ask anyone to do something I wouldn't do myself."

Like all businesses, Chris said his involves some stressors, but having family involved has helped.

"My wife, Jill, is something else," said Chris. "She has been with the business from Day One of our involvement. Jill keeps me steady, calm, and headed in the right direction. She's my mental health officer and never fails to offer the right words when times are difficult. She's just an amazing woman, and I'm very lucky to have her in my life."

Exercise also helps, he said.

"My exercise regimen was ingrained in the Army," said Chris. "We had to be up at four every morning for PT, or physical training. You cannot perform in the Army unless you're physically fit. I just kept working out every morning after leaving the service. My wife has recently begun CrossFit work outs with me every morning. She wasn't real keen on it at first, but now it's a routine for her, too."

Chris beamed when talking about his two daughters, Caroline, who is twenty-one, and Kathleen, who is eighteen.

"We're so proud of both of them," said Chris. "They have a caring spirit and are going to do some great things. They still enjoy hanging out with their Old Man, and we enjoy boating on weekends, water skiing, and hiking together."

It's a close family that still vacations together, even though Caroline Bobo, the oldest is a student at her father's alma mater, UNA. Her relationship with her dad is among the most meaningful in her life, she said.

"Dad is the kindest, smartest, and most caring man I know," said Caroline. "He's slow to anger and knows how to appropriately handle tough situations. I'm so proud of him, and I love him so much."

Chris said his fourteen years in the service helped shape the person he is today.

He also learned a valuable lesson on May 22, 1997. Captain Bobo was the platoon leader in charge of a night reconnaissance training mission at Camp Shelby, Mississippi. He was seated side-by-side in a Kiowa Warrior helicopter with fellow guard member and highly experienced pilot, Brad Green. Green was the pilot, with Chris in the co-pilot role.

The mission was routine, until, suddenly, Chris heard an unmistakable sound. He knew instantly that it was the sound of rotor blades striking tree limbs.

"I said, 'Brad, we've hit a tree,' " said Chris. "He didn't respond. It was eerie, and I wondered if maybe he'd suffered a heart attack. The helicopter suddenly began spinning out of control. It was pitch black, and, as we fell through the trees, bark and limbs began to fly through the cockpit as the helicopter ate itself up. There was nothing I could do, so I bowed my head and said a prayer. I prayed, 'God, please don't let me die.'"

The helicopter spiraled its way down and crashed onto the ground and caught fire.

"The impact knocked me unconscious, but I quickly recovered," Chris said. "I freed myself, but I couldn't locate Brad. I knew I had to find him. After repeated tries, I saw Brad in the burning wreckage and pulled him to safety. He had not survived the crash, and I've often wondered why I did."

Chris was awarded the Soldier's Medal, the highest non-combat award for heroism in the Army, for his actions following the crash.

"We just don't know for certain what's going to happen to us when we get up in the morning," Chris said. "Things happen in lives over which we have no control. The day of our accident was a normal day, just like any other. I would never have imagined that one life would be lost, and my life would be in serious jeopardy.

"So it's important to put aside worry, if possible, and embrace the good things in life. I believe it's important not to waste energy worrying about what might happen, but work to make things happen. Most of all, and I still have a hard time with this, live in the moment and enjoy what you have now."

Chapter 29

Rebekah Wright Methvin

$\mathcal{R}$ebekah is a self-described Type A personality and a recovering perfectionist. She has always been someone who believed she could control the events, both good and bad, that occur in her life. However, five years ago, she learned a lesson that literally put her on her knees, asking serious questions about why God would allow her to experience such unbearable grief. She lost her son, Mills, when he was but six weeks old, and this caused her to realize some things occur in our lives that are simply out of our control. After enduring this pain, Rebekah learned that life offered her a choice as to how she could respond to such unfathomable loss. She is featured to share what she's learned from this and other experiences.

Rebekah grew up in the Shoals as the middle daughter of a Baptist preacher. Her dad, Larry Wright, was the long-time pastor at First Baptist Church in downtown Florence, Alabama. He is now heavily involved in mission work around the globe. Her older sister, Jennifer, is a district attorney in Mobile, Alabama, while her younger sister, Stephanie, is a licensed counselor in Huntsville, Alabama. Debby Wright, the family matriarch, was responsible for keeping everyone headed in the right direction.

Rebekah graduated from Bradshaw High School in Florence and was involved in just about everything going on at the campus. She played on the high school tennis team and was a cheerleader for a couple of years as well. She was a class officer, she was on the student council, and she served as vice-president of a local social club.

She said, "I loved BHS and Auburn University for my college experience. After receiving my degree from Auburn, I heard about a job position back home in Florence. Despite not expecting to return home, I applied for and was hired by Abbott Labs in Florence."

It seemed almost too good to be true.

"I was just twenty-two, and Dennis Homan was retiring after a long and successful career as a pharmaceutical representative," Rebekah said. "Dennis served as an incredible mentor to help me learn the ins and outs of the job. I have never regretted my decision to return home. This is an amazing area with so much at our fingertips. It hurts me to see young people have to leave for job reasons."

Rebekah has worked steadily since beginning her initial career as she and husband, Roddy, have been raising a family, and being a working mom presents its own set of challenges, she said.

"I admit it's hard," Rebekah said. "All young moms are dealing with so much stress to be perfect. I try to be real and open because we're all in this same boat together. I've also tried hard to become a better listener than a talker. By listening more, I have learned that finding perfection is nothing but an illusion. We simply do the best we can."

Sharing the responsibilities with her husband helps, too, she said.

Rebekah met Rodney Methvin, whose nickname is Roddy, when he was being pastored by her dad.

"Dad met Roddy before I did," she said. "Roddy and I became friends and then began dating. We were married a few years later. Our partnership has been an incredible journey of faith. We are parents of three boys, but we lost our youngest, Mills, at the age of six weeks."

The loss has been difficult to bear, Rebekah said.

"Mills Thomas Methvin's journey began on March 20, 2010, in an unexpected emergency C-section that almost took my life," Rebekah said. "I had a placental abruption, which is when the placenta tears away from the uterus, putting mom and the baby at major risk. Mills was absolutely perfect and beautiful – just very small. On the day of his birth, we were thankful I was alive and Mills was alive. Yet deep down, we knew our journey was just beginning. While I spent the next several days recovering in ICU at ECM Hospital, Mills was transferred to the neonatal intensive care unit in Huntsville.

"Everyone told us the days in NICU were like a roller coaster – ups and downs and highs and lows. On the second night of Mills' life, he suffered a severe intraventricular hemorrhage, which is also known as bleeding on the brain. Further scans revealed his bleed to be the worst kind. The doctors didn't expect him to live much longer and wanted us to come as soon as we could to be with him. We took our first of what would be many trips to Huntsville to see Mills, and I was meeting him for the first time. Roddy and I were in complete shock, and I was trying to mentally prepare myself to say goodbye to my baby, the only time we had ever met. I wanted to tell him how sorry I was and how much I loved him. Roddy felt the same.

"But Mills was a little fighter and overcame the odds so many times during his short life. He was four weeks old before I was able to hold him in my arms. We had so many hurdles to cross, and, most days, trying to juggle our three-year-old and one-year-old at home and a baby in NICU seemed more than the strength we had to bear. We honestly had no choice but to trust God with his life. Fear threatened to overtake us, but God placed his hand on our family and kept us under his wing. So many people showed us the purest of love by sending cards, messages, and praying incessantly for our family.

"When Mills was five weeks old, the decision was made to transfer him to the NICU at Vanderbilt Children's Hospital. This began a teetering balance between praying and hoping for a miracle yet preparing for loss. We found that God's plan is bigger than our own, even though we didn't understand it. On May 1, 2010, we held Mills in our arms for the last time in a small hospital room filled with windows. We watched the rain pour down outside as if the creator of life was crying along with us. I held Mills in my arms when he took his last breath, and I felt a peace that cannot be described. It was the hardest day of our lives yet somehow the most peaceful at the same time. It was as if heaven was in that very room that day. Only God can comfort this kind of pain."

One expects to lose a parent, but losing a child can be a heart-breaking and devastating loss for a parent.

"Your heart will never be the same," said Rebekah. "This pain can only be experienced to be understood. I came to an emotional halt. I felt absolutely nothing. Everyone else was moving on, and we were consumed with overwhelming grief."

Rebekah said her faith was deeply shaken, and she admitted to being angry at God for taking her child.

"Finding a balance between profound grief and a tiny joy was a huge challenge," she said. "But over time, I came to realize that God doesn't cause our suffering; he weeps alongside us. God is who he says he is. I know that for certain. He is the one constant in life through sorrow and joy. He is the only one who can truly mend broken hearts in a broken world."

This lesson has changed the way Rebekah looks at life.

"I came to realize that much of life is out of our control," she said. "I was a Type A personality and felt I had everything planned out. But life takes twists and turns, and you can find yourself drowning. Sooner or later, we will all come to that crossroads in life. We must decide either to remain bitter or become better. I decided that I wanted to be better. I was blessed with an incredible counselor and support group during this most trying time in my life."

Her marriage, now in its twelfth year, has been rock-solid for her, she said.

"My husband has been my source of peace through the most difficult times but also the sweetest moments," Rebekah said. "I'm thankful for his adventurous spirit, his passionate heart, and how he can always make us belly laugh. The reality is that we will grieve forever over Mills, but his life, while short in time, was very important. Mills' story, that I wrote, continues to touch people's hearts and lives."

It was an experience that changed her life and continues to influence her outlook.

After ten years with Abbott Labs, and two years with Eli Lilly and Company, it was time for a change, too. Rebekah now works with Hospice of North Alabama in Florence. She has enjoyed the change of pace and direction that came with her new position. She has been working for hospice since the spring of 2013.

"I see myself making a difference in people's lives and am still using my medical background," she said. "My job is to work with the doctors and nurses in order to educate families on what hospice is and how it provides care for their loved ones. Our goal is to do everything possible to assist the patient and family during this end-of-life care. All treatment options have been exhausted when we get involved. We provide services in the home, assisted living facilities, and nursing home care. Many people avoid talking about death, but it's a necessary part of life."

While hospice has become her mission at home, Rebekah had travelled abroad to Africa as a group of three missionaries from Highland Baptist Church of Florence. Several villages there were in dire need of help, and the missionaries' purpose was to determine where best to use their resources.

She said, "It was the worst timing for me to leave my family. But life is made up of choices, and I had a distinct choice to make on this one. I felt I would miss out on a huge blessing by not going. I wanted to experience a world of instant gratification versus the all-consuming pressure of life in the United States. We are so focused on the stuff, careers, and things, none of which really matter."

At the stop in the first village, Rebekah encountered 800 orphan children. Many had yellow eyes and red hair, which are the physical hallmarks of extreme malnutrition. Many were also infected with HIV, or the virus that causes AIDS.

"The emotional impact of seeing these helpless kids made me physically sick," she said. "I felt helpless, but they were so loving and joyful, despite literally having nothing. All they had was love to give, and they thanked us so much for coming. These kids lined the streets and treated us like celebrities for coming to help them. They lived in grass huts with mud walls, and, if they were lucky, they had rice and beans to eat. They had to walk miles every day just to get water. Very few were going to school because of a lack of money. Without education, these kids have no option to improve their lives."

There were those among the group of orphans who made an impression on Rebekah.

"One young boy named Bruno became attached to me and would never leave my side," said Rebekah. "He had these dark and pleading eyes. He wanted to be close to me and sit in my lap even though he didn't know me. He loved having his picture taken as did all of the kids. They had never seen themselves before. The kids began laughing and giggling upon seeing themselves in my camera. They were overcome with joy. It was inspiring to witness such happiness over a simple photo."

What did she learn from this experience?

"These kids are happy and content with nothing," she said. "I went to bless them, but it turned out they were the ones blessing me. Life is not about the stuff, and true contentment can be found only in the heart. All they have is Jesus, and we seem to be focusing on the wrong issues and concerns."

Rebekah said her immediate family helps sponsor two children in Uganda by assisting them with money for food and education. They exchange photos and letters with each other from one side of the globe to the other. Her kids enjoy praying for them and feeling connected to the children who are so far away.

"My sons, Tate and John Walt, as well as Roddy and I, have come to realize that God loves these kids in that little country around the world as much as he does us," Rebekah said.

And that lesson guides her life today.

"A meaningful life is not about being rich, popular, being highly educated, or being perfect," she said. "It is about being real, being humble, being strong, and being able to share ourselves and touch the lives of others. It is only then that we can have a full, happy, and contented life."

Chapter 30

Clifton Billingsley

$\mathcal{M}$any of you will recognize Cliff Billingsley as the Sergeant Detective of the Florence, Alabama, Police Department who is tasked with briefing the media on local crimes, including robbery, sexual assault, and murder. Billingsley exudes a humble confidence and displays a masterful ability to remain calm and focused during a crisis. While he is reluctant to tell this story, Cliff once received the Medal of Valor for arresting a murder suspect in a fierce confrontation of the most dangerous kind. His training as a policeman and S.W.A.T. team member has given Cliff a unique perspective on life. He is included to share these lessons.

Cliff is the second son of the late Ray Billingsley and mom Gerry Billingsley. He is the father of three children, the oldest from a previous relationship, and the youngest two from his ex-wife, Ashley. Although divorced, Cliff remains very active in the lives of his children. Staying involved in his kids' lives, however, is a priority for him.

"I am a person who believes marriage is a one-time event," Cliff said. "I never expected to be in this situation, but things happen. However, without sounding corny, my ex-wife and I are probably better friends now than when we were married. We always place the children's interests ahead of our personal issues or concerns."

Being in law enforcement, Cliff has seen the ugly side of divorce.

"The jealousy, resentment, and selfishness exhibited by many couples can have dire consequences for the adults as well as the children," he said. "There will always be some friction when relationships come to an end. Through my experience, I've found it's best to put egos aside and focus on what is really important."

Before taking on the seemingly disparate roles of doting father and Sergeant Detective for the Florence Police Department, Cliff was an all-around athlete at Brooks High School.

"Don't let him fool you," said Jonathan Sparks, a high school classmate. "Cliff was an outstanding athlete. He seemed like he could float in the air forever on the basketball court."

Cliff's skill on the court allowed him to attend Northwest-Shoals Community College for two years on scholarship in 1996. After studying criminal justice at Northwest-Shoals, he pursued it as his major at the University of North Alabama. With his criminal justice degree in hand by 1998, he was hired at twenty-one as a police officer for the Florence Police Department.

Since then, Cliff has moved up the ranks to his current role.

Reflecting on his seventeen years with the force, he said, "Former Police Chief Rick Singleton initially sparked my interest in becoming an officer. He spoke at Career Day when I was a junior at Brooks High School. Chief took me on a ride-along, and I loved the aspect of helping people who couldn't protect themselves."

As one of two Sergeant Detectives in the department, Cliff oversees all personal crimes under the criminal investigation division. These crimes include assault, robbery, and murder. He remains very busy as the media liaison for the investigative division. One of the responsibilities of this role involves briefing the television and news media regarding local crimes.

"I take a lot of work off of current Police Chief Ron Tyler by handling the media," he said. "I get briefed by officers under my supervision and then brief the media."

Having seen many press conferences handled by Billingsley, the pleasing and confident tone in his voice is evident.

A bit surprisingly, the Sergeant Detective confessed that public speaking had, for a time, caused him to be nervous.

"I have always tried to be versatile and improve," he said. "I am now handling press conferences with multiple cameras pointing at me from all directions. My advice for public speaking is to step outside your comfort zone to reduce fear and improve skills."

Billingsley's position is not a desk job. In addition to his role as Sergeant Detective, he's also a member of the S.W.A.T. Team.

"My boss tells me it is really hard to get on the team and even harder to stay on it," said Cliff. "The job requires a lot of physical and mental training. Our team motto is to protect yourself and protect your buddies. Our mission is successful if we diffuse a situation without anyone being injured. Last year, our team was called out eighteen times. Surprisingly, the fatality rate of S.W.A.T. members in the line of duty is quite low. The reason is a result of the highly specialized training required to join the elite team."

Despite a very busy work schedule, Cliff has found that everyone, if so inclined, can make time in their lives for what is important. For Cliff, other than spending time with his children, that activity is exercise. Being physically fit can mean the difference between life and death for Billingsley and others in his line of work.

"I suppose most people who know me would say the Court House Racquet Club gym is my home away from home," Cliff said. "I have always kept myself in good physical condition. After my divorce several years ago, I was experiencing pain and disappointment like anyone dealing with these issues. In my business, I see many people we arrest turn to drugs or alcohol to relieve the pain. I choose to focus on improving myself physically and spiritually. It was the right choice."

Often, he sees the worst in people when performing his duties with the Florence P.D. He admitted that abuse cases involving children can be the most difficult emotionally, but hobbies help him cope.

"Other than working out at the gym, I turn to my hobbies of hiking, kayaking, and photography," he said. "This helps a lot, and the satisfaction of putting bad people in jail helps tremendously. One of the worst parts of the job is that they get out of jail too soon. Then we have to deal with them again and again."

In 2005, however, his skills, both mental and physical, were put to the test.

"I was on patrol when the call came in regarding a shooting at an apartment complex just off of Cox Creek Parkway in Florence," Cliff recalled. "Two men were seen by witnesses to have shot and killed a man during a drug deal gone wrong. I spotted their vehicle and pursued them down Mars Hill Road. Both men exited the vehicle near the Mars Hill Bible School gym and fled on foot. It was three in the morning and very dark when I began chasing one of the suspects.

"I drew my handgun, a Glock 22 .40 caliber, and attached my gun light onto the rail of my weapon. The light allowed me to keep him in my sight. He ran past the Mars Hill Day Care Center and jumped the fence; he then headed into the woods and down into a ravine. I could only see his back, so I maintained a safe distance of approximately thirty feet. He must have stopped three times because he was running out of breath. I could see he was holding something in his right hand.

"After a twenty-minute chase, he turned around, and I was face-to-face with a large man who was twice my size. I knew the suspect had just committed a murder, and he refused to obey my commands. I ordered him to get on the ground; he again refused. At this time, I was staring at him, and he was returning my glare. We were now in an area that offered a bit of light, and I noticed that he was holding his cell phone in his right hand, not a weapon. I holstered my handgun when I determined that he was unarmed. After I put away my weapon, he suddenly shouted a few obscenities, and said, 'I'll shoot you.' In the next few seconds, the suspect charged me, and we were engaged in basic hand-to-hand combat."

With a weapon in his holster, the physical violence could have, at any point, taken a dramatic turn, but Cliff said gun violence is a last option.

"I value life and try to do anything to avoid taking someone's life," he said. "Using my weapon was a last resort. I was concerned about his upper body strength pinning me on the ground. I drew my expandable baton when he attacked and hit him three times on the right thigh. I could sense he was tired, and he surrendered after about ten minutes of fighting. My superior conditioning had finally worn him down, and I got the handcuffs on him. The other suspect was not apprehended until several hours later in the early morning."

As a result of this event, Cliff was awarded the Medal of Valor, who, at great risk to himself, went above and beyond the call of duty in apprehending this murder suspect.

"I was humbled to receive such an award," he said. "I was really just performing the job that I was well-trained to do."

The career success Billingsley has had with the Florence Police Department has allowed one of his hobbies – photography – to become something of a second career in and of itself.

"I have always loved photography," he said. "I love taking photos of my children engaged in their activities. My children are my life. Some people enjoyed seeing my pictures, so I created Billingsley Photography."

Ever vigilant, Cliff seems always on alert in public situations.

"I think this goes back to my S.W.A.T. training," he said. "We're trained to focus on entire surroundings rather than have tunnel vision. This is something I tend to do even when on a date. My date might say things like 'Where are you?' Well, I'm there but am always observing whatever the situation may be."

Cliff Billingsley works in a profession that demands focus, concentration, and the ability to make split-second decisions. Sgt. Detective Billingsley is no schoolyard bully but an individual who uses his strength, training, and skills for protecting others. This need to protect has influenced how he lives his life.

As a person who sees many people from all walks of life, it seemed interesting to ask Billingsley about his definition of courage.

"I believe courage is when someone goes to the danger, or problem, when others run away," said Cliff. "This in no way means just physically but mentally as well."

The final words are left for Sgt. Detective Billingsley.

"Our actions have consequences, and someone will be affected positively or negatively by what we do," he said. "Everyone knows the difference between right and wrong. When a wrong has been committed, why not do your best to help correct it? Find the courage to do the right thing."

About the Author

ℬill Norvell was born and raised in Florence, Alabama. He graduated from Bradshaw High School in 1969 and from the University of Alabama in 1974. He currently lives in Florence with his wife, Anne, and their cat, Boo Norvell. Bill is the proud father of two sons, David Norvell and William Norvell, and two special granddaughters, Kaitlyn and Khloe Norvell.

On a dare by a friend five years ago, Bill joined the world of social networking by creating a Facebook account. Bill was surprised by the many friends he reconnected with and by the new friends he developed. The words of his seventh-grade basketball Coach Ralph Smith proved to be true as Bill recalled him saying, "You get out of something exactly what you put into it." Having put his heart into embracing friends, Bill has come to value each one of them.

Norma Glascock, one among the featured individuals, said it's important to stretch your boundaries, and to embrace new things. Bill has done so and his life has been forever enriched by the experience.